S0-BCG-431

LINCOLN'S

LAST NIGHT

LINCOLN'S

LAST NIGHT

Abraham Lincoln, John Wilkes
Booth, and the Last 36 Hours
Before the Assassination

ALAN AXELROD

Chamberlain Bros.
a member of Penguin Group (USA) Inc.
New York

CHAMBERLAIN BROS.

Published by the Penguin Group

Penguin Group (USA) Inc., 375 Hudson Street, New York, New York 10014, USA

Penguin Group (Canada), 10 Alcorn Avenue, Toronto, Ontario, Canada
M4V 3B2 (a division of Pearson Penguin Canada Inc.)

Penguin Books Ltd, 80 Strand, London WC2R 0RL, England

Penguin Ireland, 25 St Stephen's Green, Dublin 2, Ireland (a division of
Penguin Books Ltd)

Penguin Group (Australia), 250 Camberwell Road, Camberwell, Victoria
3124, Australia (a division of Pearson Australia Group Pty Ltd)

Penguin Books India Pvt Ltd, 11 Community Centre, Panchsheel Park,
New Delhi–110 017, India

Penguin Group (NZ), Cnr Airborne and Rosedale Roads, Albany, Auckland,
New Zealand (a division of Pearson New Zealand Ltd)

Penguin Books (South Africa) (Pty) Ltd, 24 Sturdee Avenue, Rosebank,
Johannesburg 2196, South Africa

Penguin Books Ltd, Registered Offices: 80 Strand, London WC2R 0RL, England

Copyright © 2005 by Alan Axelrod.

All rights reserved. No part of this book may be reproduced, scanned, or distributed in any printed or electronic form without permission. Please do not partici-
pate in or encourage piracy of copyrighted materials in violation of the author's
rights. Purchase only authorized editions. Published simultaneously in Canada.

An application has been submitted to register this book with the Library of Congress.

ISBN 1-59609-016-2

Printed in China

1 3 5 7 9 10 8 6 4 2

Book designed by Melissa Gerber
Photography from Library of Congress and The National Park Service.

CONTENTS

TICKETS

By eight that morning, Good Friday, April 14, 1865, Abraham Lincoln was at breakfast with his wife, Mary, and their sons, Tad, who was twelve, and Robert, twenty-two. The president wasn't much interested in his meal, customarily spare as it was, a single egg and a single cup of coffee. The six-foot-four Lincoln had weighed 180 pounds at his first inauguration in 1861. Now, after four years of war, he weighed a gaunt 145.

Despite his small appetite, Lincoln was intensely eager to hear what Robert had to say about the surrender of Robert E. Lee at the Appomattox Courthouse just five days earlier. He had seen it all, the two great generals, Lee and Ulysses S. Grant, meeting in the parlor of the McLean farmhouse to negotiate the terms under which the Army of Northern Virginia, beaten but unbowed, would lay down its arms. At the beginning of the year, Robert had voiced his desire to join the Union army. Mary Lincoln, who had lost two sons already—four-year-old Edward in 1850 and twelve-year-old Willie in 1862—could not bear the thought of Robert falling in battle. She begged her husband to talk him out of volunteering. Looking for a compromise, Lincoln wrote to Grant:

1

Please read this letter as though I were not President, but only a friend. My son, now in his twenty-second year, having graduated from Harvard, wishes to see something of the war before it ends. I do not wish to put him in the ranks, nor yet to give him a commission, to which those who have already served long, are better entitled, and better qualified to hold. Could he, without embarrassment to you, or detriment to the service, go into your military family with some nominal rank, and I, not the public, furnishing his necessary means? If no, say so without the least hesitation, because I am as anxious, and as deeply interested, that you shall not be encumbered as you can be yourself.

Yours truly,

A. Lincoln

Grant obligingly enrolled Robert on his staff with the rank of captain—just in time for Appomattox, as it turned out.

Robert began his narrative, only to be cut off by his mother, who had, she insisted, an *important* matter to discuss. She announced that while she already had tickets to a great gala at Grover's Theatre for that night, what she *really* wanted to see was Laura Keene—the nation's most popular comic actress—in *Our American Cousin*, at Ford's Theatre. She fixed her eyes on those of her husband, waiting for his reply.

In marrying Mary Todd in Illinois in 1842, Lincoln had known he was reaching well above his social and economic station as a struggling, self-educated country lawyer. Mary Todd, had been raised in prosperity and sophistication. Now as Mrs. Lincoln, she spent extravagantly and behaved in a manner many interpreted as haughty. Of a "nervous," "high-strung" disposition to begin with, she was prostrated by the loss of her two sons. Even in her grief, she received little sympathy from the American public. Suspicion, however, they bestowed upon her plentifully, for it was well known that her half brothers and other relatives were fighting for the Confederacy. Mary Lincoln was plagued by uncontrollable jealousies concerning her husband, as well as by nightmares, depression, and mania. During one such episode of mania, in the White House, her husband gently led her to a window that enjoyed a view of the local lunatic asylum. "Mother," he said, holding her, "if you don't stop it you will spend the rest of your days there."

Yet Abraham Lincoln never complained of his marriage to others. To one friend he remarked, "My father always said, when you make a bad bargain, hug it the tighter."

So now, as he had done on so many other occasions, Lincoln resolved to accommodate his wife. He promised her that he would attend to the tickets for that evening at Ford's. This settled (quite as she had expected), Mary Lincoln now turned to her son Robert. Would he join them? No, he replied, he had already promised to spend the evening with friends. In that case, his mother suggested, perhaps he could use the Grover's tickets—treat himself and his friends—or give them away. Turning back to her husband, she asked if she might

3

invite the Grants, Ulysses and Julia, to join them that evening. The president agreed that would be fine.

Lincoln rose from the breakfast table before nine and went to his office, located on the second floor of the White House in the southeast corner. By ten o'clock, having already seen one caller after another, he seized a spare moment to summon a messenger. He instructed him to go to Ford's Theatre, on 10th Street, between E and F, and tell the manager, James R. Ford, that he would require the "State Box" for this evening's performance. Lincoln further instructed the messenger to tell Mr. Ford that General Grant would be joining the party. Apparently, in so doing, neglect to mention Julia Grant would be there also. With the weight of Mrs. Lincoln's charge off his shoulders, the president began preparations for a cabinet meeting.

The presidential messenger reached Ford's Theatre by 10:30. James R. Ford was thrilled. Not that this was the first time the Lincolns had patronized his theater. Surviving records indicate that they had attended plays and operas there at least thirteen times before the evening of April 14, 1865. But two things *were* special about this occasion. First, the triumphant Grant would be in attendance, in truth a far bigger draw than the president himself. Second, the unexpected presence of both Grant and Lincoln was a marvelous reversal of fortune, for, even under the best of circumstances, Good Friday was not a good night for theater. Audiences were so sparse it was scarcely worth the expense of raising the curtain. And Ford knew he hardly was enjoying the best of circumstances. Miss Laura Keene was a

Laura Keene was one of America's most popular actresses during the Civil War era. She was among those who gained entry to the president's box after he was shot. "While we were waiting for Mr. Lincoln to regain strength," Dr. Leale reported, "Laura Keene appealed to me to allow her to hold the President's head. I granted the request, and she sat on the floor of the box and held his head in her lap." The actress preserved her blood-stained dress for the rest of her life.

reliable audience draw, true, as was her costar, Mr. Harry Hawk, but the evening's vehicle was thoroughly shopworn. Laura Keene had premiered *Our American Cousin* in her own New York City theater before the Civil War, back in 1858. She had purchased the American performing rights to the play from its author, Tom Taylor, a London playwright turned literature professor turned barrister turned government bureaucrat, and she was determined to get her money's worth, wringing performance after performance from what was, after all, a very slight farce. Harry Hawk's character, Asa Trenchard, an American backwoods bumpkin, goes abroad to visit his British cousins, is mistaken there for a man of wealth, and is targeted by a Mrs. Mountchessington as a good catch for her marriageable daughter, Augusta.

It was bad enough that on Good Friday Ford had nothing more exciting than a burned out old warhorse to offer. Worse, C. Dwight Hess, who managed Ford's main competition, Grover's Theatre, was staging a genuine spectacle that night. It was a brand-new play, *Aladdin, or the Wonderful Lamp*, and it was only one part of what Grover's was billing as a "monster victory celebration," which included a spectacular display of lights and a roster of songs specially composed for the occasion. Withal, it had promised to be a grim evening for Ford's Theatre. But now, like heroes of hoary melodrama, Grant and Lincoln suddenly rode to the rescue. Mr. Ford may or may not have given Lincoln's messenger actual tickets to the performance, but he certainly and smilingly assured him that the State Box would be in readiness, with the president's favorite rocking chair in place, and that the management would be honored by the presence of such distinguished guests.

Abraham Lincoln loved the theater and was a frequent guest at Ford's. On April 14, 1865, the president and his party were accommodated in the "State Box," which actually consisted of two adjoining boxes. When he leaped to the stage after shooting Lincoln and tangling with Major Rathbone, Booth caught his spur on the banner festooning the box farther from the stage. This caused him to land awkwardly on one foot, breaking the small bone in his left leg a few inches above the ankle.

A number of historians have written that Abraham Lincoln was reluctant to go to the theater that night and went only to please his wife. Full of foreboding, the reluctance surely adds to the drama of April 14, but there is, in fact, no evidence to support it. Lincoln had loved the theater ever since his youth in New Salem, Illinois, where the local blacksmith, Jack Kelso, introduced him to the plays of William Shakespeare. The Bard became a lifelong favorite of Lincoln's, and he committed entire plays to memory. The profundity of the tragedies especially appealed to him, and he found both illumination and solace in such figures as Hamlet, Lear, and, most of all, Macbeth, his favorite character in his favorite play. Yet he also reveled in the comic figure of Falstaff in *Henry IV*. Too, his theatrical taste was hardly confined to Shakespeare. On November 9, 1863, for example, the president sat in the State Box at Ford's to see a performance of a popular play about Raphael, *The Marble Heart*, by Charles Selby. The great artist of the Italian Renaissance was portrayed by a darkly handsome matinee idol named John Wilkes Booth.

So there is every reason to believe that Abraham Lincoln, eating his single breakfast egg and sipping his single cup of coffee, sickened by war and thirty-five pounds underweight, was happy enough to oblige his wife with a soothing night of empty-headed comedy. And we may also assume he was pleased to end Mary's interruption of Robert's account of Appomattox. As the young man resumed his narrative, he presented his father with a little gift—a picture of Robert E. Lee—which he gave to the president as a kind of lighthearted joke. But Lincoln, affixing his glasses on his nose, studied the image intently and without smiling.

"It is a good face," he said. "I am glad the war is over at last."

Much like her husband, Mary Todd Lincoln was subject to fits of near mania alternating with spells of suicidal melancholy. She endured the deaths of her three-year-old son Edward in 1850, her second son, Willie, in 1862, her husband, who was murdered at her very side in 1865, and her youngest son, Tad, in 1875. Her surviving son, Robert Todd Lincoln, caused her to be committed to a private sanatorium in Batavia, Illinois, the year Tad died, but she was released a few months later. After a sojourn in Europe, she returned to Springfield, Illinois, in 1880 and died there two years later. She was buried beside her husband at Springfield's Oak Ridge Cemetery.

DREAMS

enerations of schoolbook histories have portrayed Robert E. Lee's surrender at Appomattox on April 9, 1865, as the end of the Civil War. It is true that Lee's Army of Northern Virginia, long the chief military instrument of the Confederacy, had suddenly ceased to exist, but some 175,000 other Confederate soldiers had yet to wave the white flag. The two largest remaining contingents were an army under the command of Joseph E. Johnston in North Carolina, about 89,000 troops, and approximately 50,000 men under Major General Kirby Smith west of the Mississippi. Yet the importance of Appomattox escaped no one in the North, and if further proof were required that the war was over in spirit, if not finally in deed, it came on April 14. Four years earlier, in Charleston Harbor, Major Robert Anderson had surrendered Fort Sumter to his former West Point artillery student, Confederate general P. G. T. Beauregard, after enduring two days and nights of continuous bombardment. Now, on the fourteenth, Brigadier General Anderson was scheduled to raise the Stars and Stripes over Fort Sumter, at 11:12 A.M., four years to the minute after having been lowered in disgrace.

In Washington, it was this event that Grover's Theatre planned to celebrate with *Aladdin*, the songs, and the display of lights, reflecting the sentiment of many Northerners, that raising the flag once again over Sumter truly signified the end of the war. Although he was well aware that armies were still in the field, Abraham Lincoln was apparently among those who saw April 14 as the last day of the great struggle. Later this afternoon, Mary would remark on her husband's "great cheerfulness," and Lincoln would reply: "Mary, I consider *this day*, the war has come to a close." But it was not the impending ceremony at Fort Sumter nor the atmosphere of jubilation on the streets of Washington that made for the president's cheerful mood on this day. He had awakened with it.

The night had been an unusually peaceful one for Lincoln, who arose at seven o'clock, which was late for this habitual early riser. He awakened from a dream he considered so auspicious that he shared it with his cabinet and General Grant later in the day.

While April 14 was unquestionably a day of joy, there hovered over it an unanswered question: *When would William Tecumseh Sherman send word that Joe Johnston and his large army had surrendered?* This would be the penultimate death knell for the Confederacy. At about eleven, during a cabinet meeting— at which Grant was a guest—one of the secretaries asked if anyone had heard anything from Sherman. Grant answered that he expected some word within an hour or two. At this, President Lincoln quietly announced that he *knew* it would be good news.

How did he know this?

Because of his dream from the night before. It was a

12

recurring dream, he explained, one that always preceded some great event in the war.

"What kind of dream was it?" asked Gideon Welles, secretary of the navy.

"It relates to your element," Lincoln answered, "the water. I seemed to be in some singular, indescribable vessel and I was moving with great rapidity toward an indefinite shore."

In the face of what we know would happen to Lincoln that night, the image of drifting rapidly toward "an indefinite shore" hardly seems to bode well. Perhaps Lincoln's cabinet was also puzzled by the president's cheerful interpretation of the imagery. In any case, Lincoln hastily added: "I had this dream preceding Sumter, and Bull Run, Antietam, Gettysburg, Stone River, Vicksburg and Wilmington."

If the others remained politely silent, General Grant, ever the realist, offered: "Stone River was certainly no victory, nor can I think of any great results following it."

Indeed, the general might have pointed out the even more obvious facts that the fall of Fort Sumter and both battles of Bull Run were unmitigated Union disasters. As for Antietam, it was a Union victory so narrow that most historians consider it a draw and all agree that it was the single bloodiest day of the war.

Lincoln acknowledged Grant's point about Stone River, but he repeated nevertheless that the dream portended good news. "I had this strange dream again last night," he repeated, "and we shall, judging from the past, have great news very soon. I think it must be from Sherman. My thoughts are in that direction."

Especially "judging from the past," Lincoln's insistence that the dream boded well is puzzling, but we can hardly begrudge him his rare good thoughts on the morning of April 14. No American president has borne so great a burden as Lincoln, and the Civil War, with more than 1.1 million casualties on both sides—more than a fifth of the nation's men of military age—remains by far the costliest war in American history. And now, at last, it was clearly coming to an end.

Even apart from the war, Lincoln was by nature often a melancholy man, given to periods of profound depression. One of his early colleagues in the Illinois state legislature, Robert L. Wilson, recalled a conversation that had occurred about 1836: Lincoln "told me that although he appeared to enjoy life rapturously, still he was the victim of terrible melancholy. He sought company, and indulged in fun and hilarity without restraint, or stint as to time. Still when by himself, he told me that he was so overcome with mental depression, that he never dare carry a knife in his pocket. As long as I was intimately acquainted with him . . . he never carried a pocket knife." Lincoln's courtship of Mary Todd had been turbulent, and, on January 1, 1841, he even broke his engagement to her. From January 13 to 19, he was unable to attend the ongoing session of the Illinois state legislature, almost certainly because of debilitating depression. On January 23, he wrote to his first law partner, John T. Stuart: "I am now the most miserable man living. If what I feel were equally distributed to the whole human family, there would not be one cheerful face on the earth. Whether I shall ever be better I can not tell; I awfully forebode I shall not. To remain as I am is impossible; I must die or be better, it appears to me." Some years later, his third law partner, William Herndon, remarked that "his melancholy dripped from him as he walked. . . . He was gloomy, abstracted, and joyous—rather humorous—by turns; but I do not think he knew what real joy was for many years." A boyhood friend, James Grigsby, recalled that, even as a child, Lincoln would "get fits of blues . . . for two or three days at a time."

In the White House, Abraham Lincoln longed for happy dreams, but, like his wife, chronically suffered from nightmares. William H. Crook, an officer of Washington's Metropolitan Police assigned as one of Lincoln's bodyguards, sometimes drew night duty and recalled in his 1907 memoir the chilling sound of the president moaning in his sleep. "I would stand there [outside his bedroom door] and listen," Crook wrote, "until a sort of panic stole over me."

On the evening of Tuesday, April 11, 1865, the president and Mrs. Lincoln entertained a few friends in the Red Room of the White House. Tea and cakes were served at ten, after which most of the guests bade their host and hostess good night. Only James Harlan, his daughter Mary, John P. Usher, Ward Hill Lamon, and one or two others remained. Harlan was one of Iowa's senators and now secretary-designate of the Department of the Interior. A good friend of the Lincoln family, his daughter would later marry Robert Lincoln. Usher was the outgoing Interior secretary, having tendered his resignation in order to become a high-paid lawyer for the Union Pacific. Lamon had been Lincoln's informal law partner from 1852 to 1856 and had campaigned for him in his 1854 and 1858 Senate runs and then in the 1860 presidential election. During the perilous inaugural journey from Springfield, Illinois, to

Washington in 1861, Lamon served his close friend as a bodyguard, and, once arrived in the capital, he was appointed marshal for the city of Washington and chief of protocol at the White House.

Lamon recalled, word for word, the turn the conversation suddenly took after Mrs. Lincoln remarked that, while so many others were jubilant following Appomattox, her husband's face looked long and sad.

"It seems strange," Lincoln said, as if in response to his wife's observation, "how much there is in the Bible about dreams. There are, I think, some sixteen chapters in the Old Testament and four or five in the New in which dreams are mentioned; and there are many other passages scattered throughout the book which refer to visions. If we believe the Bible, we must accept the fact that, in the old days, God and his angels came to men in their sleep and made themselves known in dreams." Perhaps suddenly self-conscious, he continued in a different vein: "Nowadays, dreams are regarded as very foolish, and are seldom told, except by old women and by young men and maidens in love."

As Abraham Lincoln had, through the years, grown all too familiar with the signs of emotional instability in his wife, so Mary Lincoln knew the signs that portended her husband's attacks of melancholia. In some alarm now, she asked, "Why? Do you believe in dreams?"

Lincoln caught himself up.

"I can't say that I do." Then he continued: "But I had one the other night which has haunted me ever since. After it occurred, the first time I opened the Bible, strange as it may appear, it was at the twenty-eighth chapter of Genesis, which relates the wonderful dream Jacob had. I turned to other passages, and seemed to encounter a dream or a vision wherever I looked. I kept on turning the leaves of the old book, and everywhere my eyes fell upon passages recording matters strangely in keeping with my own thoughts—supernatural visitations, dreams, visions, and so forth."

"You frighten me." Mary nearly gasped. "What is the matter?"

Again, Lincoln *tried* to back off.

"I am afraid that I have done wrong to mention the subject at all." Yet he could not help himself. "But somehow, the thing has gotten possession of me, and, like Banquo's ghost, it will not down."

Frightened as she was, Mrs. Lincoln insisted that he tell the dream.

Lamon recalled that Lincoln began, "About ten days ago"—which would have put the dream on the night of April 1; however, this close friend of the president's believed the dream had actually occurred on March 19, after the Lincolns attended a performance of Charles Gounod's opera *Faust*—"I retired very late. I had been waiting up for important dispatches. I could not have been long in bed when I fell into a slumber, for I was weary. I soon began to dream. There seemed to be a deathlike stillness about me. Then I heard subdued sobs, as if a number of people were weeping. I thought I left my bed and wandered downstairs.

"There the silence was broken by the same pitiful sobbing, but the mourners were invisible. I went from room to room. No living person was in sight, but the same mournful sounds of distress met me as I passed along. It was light in all the rooms; every object was familiar to me, but where were all the people who were grieving as if their hearts would break?

"I was puzzled and alarmed. What could be the meaning of all this? Determined to find the cause of a state of things so mysterious and so shocking, I kept on until I arrived in the East Room, which I entered. There I met with a sickening surprise. Before me was a catafalque, on which rested a corpse in funeral vestments. Around it were stationed soldiers who were acting as guards; and there was a throng of people, some gazing mournfully upon the corpse, whose face was covered, others weeping pitifully.

" 'Who is dead in the White House?' I demanded of one of the soldiers.

" 'The president,' was his answer. 'He was killed by an assassin.'

"Then came a loud burst of grief from the crowd, which awoke me from my dream. I slept no more that night, and, although it was only a dream, I have been strangely annoyed by it ever since."

Lamon recalled a dead silence of several minutes following this narration, broken finally by Mrs. Lincoln: "That is horrid. I wish you had not told it. I am glad I don't believe in dreams, or I should be in terror from this time forth."

Perhaps having delivered himself of the dream's heavy weight, Lincoln actually smiled: "It was only a dream, Mother. Let us say no more about it, and try to forget it."

Understandably, it was at this point that the Lincolns' remaining guests made to leave. John Usher and Ward Lamon lingered a moment, to dissuade the president from venturing outside of the White House after dark. Lincoln asked Lamon to go to Richmond, the fallen capital of the Confederacy, to represent him at a state convention there. Lamon agreed to go but again beseeched Lincoln not to go out until he had returned.

"Usher," Lincoln said playfully, "this boy is a monomaniac on the subject of my safety. I can hear him, or hear of his being around, at all times of the night, to prevent somebody from murdering me. He thinks I shall be killed, and we think he is going crazy." Taking his good friend Lamon by the shoulders, he shook him gently. "What does anybody want to assassinate me for? If anyone wants to do so, he can do it any day or night, if he is ready to give his life for mine. It is nonsense."

But Usher sided with Lamon on this matter, and Lamon cited the dream the president had just related.

"Don't you see how it will turn out?" Lincoln countered. "In this dream it was not me but some other fellow that was killed. It seems that this ghostly assassin tried his hand on someone else."

The president forced a laugh.

"And that reminds me," he continued, "of an old farmer in Illinois whose family was made sick by eating greens. Some poisonous herb had got into the mess, and members of the family were in danger of dying. There was a half-witted boy in the family called Jake, and always afterward when they had greens the old man would say: 'Now, afore we risk these greens, let's try them on Jake. If he stands them, we're all right.'

"Just so with me. As long as this imaginary assassin continues to exercise himself on others, I can stand it."

No one laughed except the president.

"Well," he said, "let it go. I think the Lord in His own good time and way will work this out all right. God knows what is best."

People who knew Lincoln, as well as those who later wrote about him, typically reported that the president was "fatalistic" on the subject of assassination. That was true enough. "*If anyone wants to kill me*," Lincoln had said, "he can do it any day or night, if he is ready to give his life for mine." But it is also true that Lincoln was in denial where assassination was concerned: "What does anybody want to assassinate me for?" The dream about a dead president in the White House, he insisted, concerned "some other fellow." A modern psychiatrist would doubtless diagnose Lincoln as manic-depressive or bipolar. Jonathan Birch, an Illinois lawyer, remembered Lincoln in court: "His eyes would sparkle with fun, and when he had reached the point in his narrative which invariably evoked the laughter of the crowd, nobody's enjoyment was greater than his. An hour later he might be seen in the same place or in some law office nearby, but, alas, how different! His chair, no longer in the center of the room, would be leaning back against the wall; his feet drawn up and resting on the front rounds so that his knees and chair were about on a level; his hat tipped slightly forward as if to shield his face; his eyes no longer sparkling with fun or merriment, but sad and downcast and his hands clasped around his knees. There, drawn up within himself as it were, he would sit, the very picture of dejection and gloom. . . . No one ever thought of breaking the spell by speech; for by his moody silence and abstraction he had thrown about him a barrier so dense and impenetrable no one dared to break through." His attitude toward assassination was very much of a piece with this—utterly ambivalent, by turns fatalistically resigned, then breezily dismissive.

He arose at seven that morning, April 14, 1865, and emerged from his bedroom, at the southwest corner of the second floor of the White House, into the hall that connected it with his office at the southeast corner. There was always a guard or two in the hall, and Lincoln always bade the men good morning, but even at this early hour, and even earlier still, the hall swarmed with men the guards seemed incapable of keeping out. They were petitioners of every stripe, looking for patronage jobs, looking for passes through the Union lines to do business in the South, looking for special favors, for pardons, for redress of myriad grievances. Any of these men easily could have concealed a derringer or dagger. For Lincoln's part, he did his best to ignore them. If one proved particularly insistent, the president would apologize: "Sorry. I cannot help you." His belief was that only people whose appeals had been rejected by the proper authorities were desperate enough to call on him here and he was not about to circumvent the legitimate authority of his own government.

Leaving behind the blended murmur of grumbling men and even those who wept in frustration in his wake, Abraham Lincoln finally reached his office, nodded to the soldier who guarded it, and walked inside.

Near the south windows of the office, opposite the door, was the president's pigeonhole desk. In one of these "special pigeonholes," according to his secretary John Hay, Lincoln kept a "bulging folder" in which he had collected some eighty letters over the past four years. They were all death threats, or, rather, they were the threats he chose to save among the many he routinely received. Did he save them out of fear? Was he collecting evidence for his guards or the police? Was he morbidly fascinated by the venomous tone of those letters? Or was he simply amused by them? Perhaps their very existence somehow made him feel *more* secure. Elizabeth Keckley, Mary Lincoln's seamstress and one of her few confidants, reported that the president treated the death threats lightly, claiming that no one would be silly enough to write a letter announcing his plan to kill the president. Perhaps Lincoln viewed the letters as evidence that there were at least eighty or so people who would *never* try to kill him.

If the president looked up from his desk and out the window, he would have seen a misty, chilly morning in which the sun struggled to be even a wan ghost of itself. On his desk was the document appointing one William T. Howell Indian agent for Michigan. The president had made the appointment some five weeks earlier, but instead of "distributing" it now, to make it official, he appended to it a message to commissioner of Indian affairs William P. Dole: "Please do not send off the Commission of W. T. Howell, as Indian agent in Michigan, until the return of Mr. Harlan, and hearing from me again." He signed the note: "Yours truly, A. Lincoln." James Harlan, former senator from Iowa, one of the intimate group privy to the president's dream had been confirmed as the new secretary of the interior on March 9, the day before Lincoln signed Howell's commission. Lincoln now thought it prudent to affirm Harlan's authority by giving *him* the opportunity to approve—or deny—Howell's appointment after formally assuming office, which would occur in just a few days.

After attending to the Howell matter, Lincoln opened a letter from James H. Van Alen, a New York friend. It warned the president to "guard his life" and to avoid exposing himself "to assassination as he had by going to Richmond" on April 4, after Union troops had taken the city. Lincoln took paper and pen and wrote a reply, which began, "My dear Sir: I intend to adopt the advice of my friends and use due precaution . . ."

Setting aside correspondence now, the president, in the dim and misty light, would have had to turn up the gaslight to begin his next regular early morning task: reading the newspapers laid out on a table beside the desk. Some papers were brutally and consistently hostile to the administration, others were supportive. Lincoln read them all. They were served, collectively, as a means for him to keep his finger on the pulse of the nation. Turning from the desk, with its pigeonholed letters, he would take a paper from the table, sit with it in the high-backed chair near the gaslight, and start reading.

WALLET

ecovered from the pockets of Abraham Lincoln's long black frock coat after his death were two pairs of spectacles together with a lens polisher, a pocketknife (oddly enough), a watch fob, a linen handkerchief, and a brown leather wallet. Inside the wallet were a five-dollar Confederate note and eight newspaper clippings. All of these items were given to Robert Lincoln, and they remained in the Lincoln family until 1937, when the president's granddaughter, Mary Lincoln Isham, presented them to the Library of Congress. Because the library traditionally dealt only with books and documents, the contents of the president's pockets were not put on display until 1976. Since then, they have been among the pieces library visitors most often ask to see.

Think of your own wallet. You put into it things that are very important day to day—cash, credit cards, driver's license—and things that are important lifelong: paramountly, pictures of family. We can only wonder why Lincoln chose to put a Confederate note and newspaper clippings into his wallet.

The Confederate note might have served to remind him of both the reality and the enormity of secession. After all, each

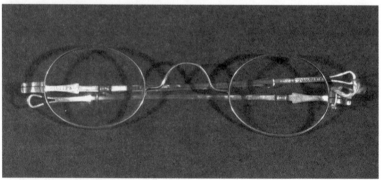

These eyeglasses, their case, and a lens cleaner were among the personal items the president carried on the last night of his life.

piece of currency a government prints is a bold declaration of its legitimacy and its right to exist. Lincoln might also have regarded it as a token of humanity of the "enemy." No government document is more intimate, after all, than its currency, which passes from hand to hand and is used to purchase the necessities of life itself.

As for the newspaper clippings, we must assume they held some real importance for the president. An indefatigable reader of the news, it is likely he clipped them himself as he sat in his high-backed chair beside his pigeonhole desk. Their content varies.

The two earliest clippings, both from 1863, can best be summarized by what the headline of one called "The Disaffection Among Southern Soldiers." That article reprinted a letter found by Union troops in the streets of Brandon, Mississippi. Dated July 16, 1863, written after the fall of Vicksburg to Union forces on July 4, it reflects the general dissolution of the Confederacy in the West and the effect of Lincoln's controversial Emancipation Proclamation:

> Ruin, utter and entire ruin, has swept over this State. The negro emancipation policy, at which we so long hooted, is the most potent lever of our overthrow. It steals upon us unawares, and ere we can do anything the plantations are deserted, families without servants, camps without necessary attendants, women and children in want and misery. In short, the disadvantages to us now arising from the negroes are ten-fold greater than have been all the advantages derived from earlier in the war. . . certainly we are a defeated and a ruined

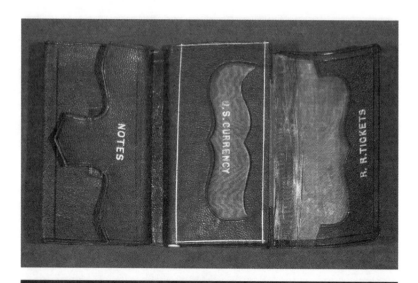

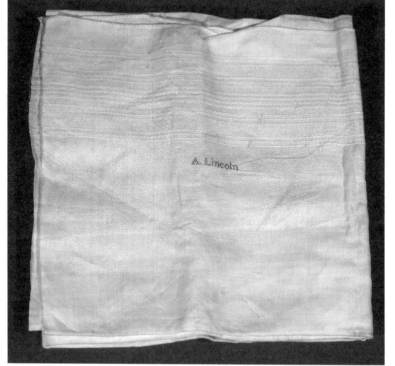

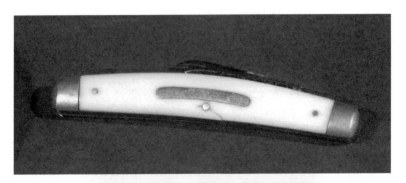

The night he was killed, President Lincoln carried this wallet, linen handkerchief, and pocket knife.
Pictured here is the fob of the president's watch.

people, shorn of our strength, powerless . . .

The second article, headlined "A Conscript's Epistle to Jeff. Davis," reprinted a letter found by Union troops in an abandoned Confederate camp in North Carolina. In language both flowery and acidic, the writer curses the Confederate president who drafted him, concluding with: "Your happy conscript would go to the far-away North whence the wind comes, and leave you to reap the whirlwind, with no one but your father, the Devil, to rake and bind after you. . . . And now, bastard President of a political abortion, farewell. . . . Except it be in the army of the Union, you will not again see the conscript, NORM. HARROLD, of Ashe county, N.C."

Another three clippings, dating from 1864, concern what was then the upcoming presidential election, in which Lincoln was running for reelection against former Union general George B. McClellan. "The Two Platforms" includes the official platforms of Lincoln's Republican Party and McClellan's Democrats. Whereas the Republicans would accept nothing less than total victory, including restoration of the Union and the unconditional abolition of slavery, the Democratic platform called for "immediate efforts . . . for the cessation of hostilities" and "peace [to be] restored on the basis of the Federal Union of the States"—in other words, a negotiated settlement with the South. Along with this clipping, Lincoln included one headed "John Bright on the Presidency." Bright, a British Quaker politician and social reformer, had dedicated himself to countering the powerful pro-Confederate sympathies that were pervasive throughout Great Britain. As a Quaker, Bright was passionately opposed to slavery and was an enthusiastic supporter of Abraham Lincoln. He wrote to Horace Greeley, editor of the New York *Tribune*:

> All those of my countrymen who have wished well to the rebellion . . . who have preferred a Southern Slave Empire rather than a restored and free Republic . . . are now in favor of the election of Gen. McClellan. All those who have deplored the calamities which the leaders of secession have brought upon your country who believe that Slavery weakens your power and tarnishes your good name throughout the world . . . are heartily longing for the re-election of Mr. Lincoln.

Additional praise came from the Reverend Henry Ward Beecher, America's most prominent religious leader, whose speech at Philadelphia's Academy of Music is quoted in an article headed simply "President Lincoln." Citing the example of the seventh president, a universally popular hero, Beecher observed: "Abraham Lincoln may be a great deal less testy and wilful than Andrew Jackson, but in a long race, I do not know but that he will be equal to him." (On April 14, 1865, at a ceremony honoring the raising of the Stars and Stripes at Fort Sumter once again, the same Henry Ward Beecher would make a speech in which he thanked God for having sustained the life of the president "under the unparalleled burdens and sufferings of four bloody years, and permitted him to behold this auspicious confirmation of that national unity for which he has waited with so much patience and fortitude.")

An article headed "Sherman's Orders for His March. Special Field Order—No.120 . . . Nov. 9, 1864," reprinted the orders William T. Sherman issued governing his controversial and supremely destructive March to the Sea, which was directed against the civilian population of the South and which was intended, in Sherman's words, to "make Georgia howl." The orders include an admonition to observe a kind of rough justice as opposed to military lawlessness: "In districts and neighborhoods where the army is unmolested, no destruction . . . should be permitted, but should guerillas or bushwhackers molest our march . . . then army corps commanders should order and enforce a devastation more or less relentless, according to the measure of such hostility."

The most recent articles found in Abraham Lincoln's wallet were a pair reporting on Missouri's state constitutional convention of January 1865. Missouri was a deeply divided state, in which pro-slavery and abolitionist factions had clashed violently even before the Civil War began. The state never seceded, yet, throughout the war, it was the scene of intensely bitter guerrilla fighting. Late in the war, Radical Republicans pressed Lincoln to force Missouri to enact immediate emancipation, and they accused the governor, Hamilton Rowan Gamble, of being a "copperhead"—a pro-Confederate Northerner. The president, whose Emancipation Proclamation of January 1, 1863, freed slaves in the Confederacy only but not in "Border States" like Missouri, which, though slaveholding, were still part of the Union, approved of Missouri freeing its slaves at its own pace. This move drew intense criticism from the radicals within Lincoln's own party. One article, headlined "Emancipation in

Missouri," reprinted the "Ordinance of Emancipation" adopted by the Missouri state convention, which called for phased abolition to be completed entirely by July 4, 1870. The other article, "The Message of the Governor of Missouri," published the following day, presents a point of view that must have greatly gratified Lincoln:

> Slavery is dead in Missouri. That vast State, the geographical center of the Republic, may henceforth be set down as a free State. But the [Northern] radicals are not satisfied with the death of slavery. Like the boy who pounded the dead snake, they want to "make it *deader*." And we have no objections to any blows inflicted upon the institution. But because the President did not yield to demands of the radicals that seemed intolerant and obtrusive, he is charged by hundreds of furious journalists with deserting "the cause of freedom." The charge is unfounded and absurd. Doubtless he would rejoice as heartily as any radical, at the speedy abolition of slavery in Missouri, but he is not disposed to encourage excesses that might damage the good cause itself.

If the death threats Abraham Lincoln chose to pigeonhole represented the most extreme form of criticism of his administration, the clippings he chose to save furnished vindication. Yet none of them is lavish in praise of the president. Instead, the content of the articles is factual, what a lawyer—and Lincoln was a very good lawyer—would call "evidentiary." There were two letters from disgruntled rebel soldiers, evidence of the illegitimacy and dissolution of the Confederacy; there was the platform of Lincoln versus the platform of McClellan; there were unsolicited testimonials from the prominent Britisher John Bright and the prominent American Henry Ward Beecher; there was the stern justice of Sherman's marching orders; and there was vindication of Lincoln's moderate policy in the all-important case of Missouri. Capable of finding reassurance even in the most dubious of dreams, Lincoln also sought comfort in the rigorous evidence of fact. An avid reader of newspapers, he passed over the many articles of empty pro-administration puffery as well as the many articles of anti-administration vituperation; instead, he chose to clip and save only facts, facts that were comforting to him precisely in proportion to their factual rigor.

VISITORS

A braham Lincoln attended to correspondence and read the
newspapers until he was called into breakfast around eight
o'clock. After eating his egg, drinking his coffee, promising
Mrs. Lincoln that he would see about getting tickets to *Our
American Cousin*, and listening to Robert talk about Appomattox, he
rose from the table and announced that he had to get back to work.
Returning to his office, he resumed reading newspapers and official
correspondence and signed two documents before he looked up,
shortly after nine, and nodded to the soldier who served as his office
doorkeeper to admit the first visitor of the morning.

He was brown-bearded Schuyler Colfax, Speaker of the
House. Taking the Speaker's hand, the president declared
smilingly, "Bob has just returned home and breakfasted with us.
He was at the surrender of Lee, and told me that some of the
rebel officers told him they were very glad the contest was over
at last." Beyond this, no one knows for certain what Lincoln and
Colfax discussed. Colfax, who as vice president during Ulysses S.
Grant's first term in the White House would be deeply
implicated in the infamous Crédit Moblier transcontinental

Robert Todd Lincoln, eldest son of Abraham and Mary, was summoned to the president's deathbed at the Petersen house. He recovered from the trauma of his father's loss to become a millionaire corporation attorney and also served as U.S. secretary of war under James A. Garfield and Chester A. Arthur, who took office after Garfield fell victim to an assassin's bullet. Later, Lincoln was appointed minister to Great Britain.

railroad financing scandal in 1872, impressed Lincoln as pragmatic at best and something of a self-serving scoundrel at worst. Yet he was a likable man, and, as Speaker of the House, was highly useful to the president. It is likely that the two discussed his possible appointment to the cabinet, perhaps to replace Secretary of War Edwin M. Stanton, who craved appointment to the Supreme Court. It is also likely that Colfax pressed Lincoln for a promise that postwar policy toward the South—"Reconstruction"—would not be formulated without calling Congress into special session. Members of the House as well as the Senate were concerned that Lincoln would take advantage of the current congressional recess to dictate policy through a rapid-fire series of executive orders. In fact, it was precisely this that Lincoln had in mind, and the only promise he could offer Colfax was that while he had "no intention at the moment" of calling a special session, he would "give the due sixty days' notice" if "I change my mind."

Schuyler Colfax left, less in frustration over having failed to secure the promise he sought on behalf of Congress presumably, than self-satisfied that a cabinet appointment was indeed in the offing for himself. Doubtless, as he passed into the hall, he smiled a greeting to the president's next visitor, Congressman Cornelius Cole of California. No record exists of the substance of this meeting, but, during it, Lincoln probably had his eye on the clock since the regular Friday cabinet meeting—even on Good Friday—was to begin at eleven sharp and the president had more visitors waiting, including Detroit lawyer William Alanson Howard and former New Hampshire senator John P. Hale.

As is the case with Cornelius Cole, it is impossible to guess

39

the subject of the president's conversation with William Howard. As for John Hale, however, it is likely that the meeting concerned matters of state, for the president had just appointed him the nation's new minister (the equivalent of ambassador) to Spain. Hale was especially grateful for this because, after sixteen years in the Senate, he had been defeated in his bid for reelection. It is known that at this meeting Lincoln advised Hale to work closely with Frederick Seward, assistant secretary of state under his father, William H. Seward, who was undergoing a painful convalescence from severe injuries suffered in a carriage accident, and because he was bedridden, was in no condition at present to deal with the affairs of his department. What is not known is whether Hale mentioned to Lincoln what he had already confided to a few friends: that he was greatly relieved to be taking himself and his family out of the country at just this moment because his daughter, Lucy Lambert Hale, was becoming seriously involved in a romance with an actor by the name of John Wilkes Booth. (Some historians have suggested that, for her part at least, Lucy considered herself Booth's fiancée; Booth's sister, Asia, noted only that her brother had sent Lucy a valentine poem on February 14, 1865. Whatever the degree of his involvement with her, Booth, an outspoken pro-slavery white supremacist, must have known that Lucy's Radical Republican father was an ardent abolitionist.)

In a brief interval between one morning visitor and the next, Lincoln acted on his wife's wishes, summoning and sending a messenger to Ford's Theatre, so that he could now focus all of his attention on the eleven o'clock cabinet meeting.

CABINET

They filed into the Cabinet Room in succession: Secretary of the Navy Gideon Welles, Assistant Secretary of State Frederick Seward, Postmaster General William Dennison, Attorney General James Speed, outgoing Secretary of the Interior John P. Usher (James Harlan had not yet assumed office), Secretary of the Treasury Hugh McCulloch, and, late as usual, Secretary of War Edwin Stanton, who had a guest in tow, General Ulysses S. Grant. Lincoln greeted each as they arrived, and each found the president's cheerful mood perfectly appropriate to the day—indeed, to the very hour. For just twelve minutes after the cabinet meeting began, the American flag was being raised once again over Fort Sumter in Charleston Harbor.

Although the topic for the meeting was pressing—nothing less than the policy for Reconstruction—the president relished informal conversation with each member he greeted, and he took extra time to inquire of Frederick Seward about the health of his father. Then when he stood to shake the hand of General Grant, the entire assembly broke into spontaneous applause, which the president permitted all to savor. Notably absent was Vice President Andrew Johnson. Nobody much liked him, with his graceless manner and his grating protestations of his humble origins, unctuously and habitually repeated in the manner of *David Copperfield*'s Uriah Heep. So he simply wasn't invited.

When, at last, all were seated at the green baize-topped cabinet table, the president continued to resist plunging into the matter of Reconstruction. His first question was to Grant: Was there any news from Sherman concerning the surrender of Joe Johnston's big army? No, there was none, but he expected word in an hour or two. At this, Lincoln began to relate his dream about sailing rapidly in an "indescribable vessel" toward "an indefinite shore," but interrupted himself to turn the meeting at last to the hard work of Reconstruction policy. Edwin Stanton quickly interjected that, barring disagreement, he intended to announce an immediate end to the military draft. Not only would this universally raise spirits, it would unambiguously signal an end to the war while also beginning to stanch the wartime hemorrhage of government funds. On the latter subject, Stanton added that he had assigned General Grant to start the enormous task of bringing the war machinery to a halt through the orderly canceling of government contracts and the rapid demobilization of the army.

All agreed with Stanton and the matter was quickly settled. Then Lincoln again turned to Reconstruction. Frederick Seward chimed in with a report of his morning's discussion with his father, William. Nine days earlier, on April 5, the sixty-four-year-old had suffered a skull fracture, broken jaw, broken arm, and assorted contusions and lacerations when his two-horse team ran away with his carriage, struck a curb, and overturned. Flat on his back, William found it painful to speak, even in a whisper, but

Vice President Andrew Johnson, unpolished, uncouth, and unpopular, became president on Lincoln's death. In 1868, he survived an impeachment trial by a single vote in the Senate.

speak he did, advising president and cabinet through Frederick that the Treasury should assume immediate control of all Southern customs houses and begin the collection of revenues; that the War Department should immediately garrison or destroy all Southern forts; that the Department of the Navy without delay should dispatch armed vessels to drop anchor in all Southern ports and take possession of all navy yards, ships, and ordnance; that Interior should immediately dispatch Indian agents, pension agents, land agents, and surveyors to reassess Southern territory; that the Post Office Department should hasten to reopen all post offices and reestablish all mail routes; and that the attorney general should quickly appoint needed judges and reopen the courts throughout the South.

The absent Seward's torrent of directives spurred lively discussion, with Stanton rushing to take the lead by presenting his own comprehensive—as well as dictatorial and punitive—plan for Reconstruction.

Waving the document he had composed, Edwin Stanton promised: "I will see that each of you gets a copy of this."

Lincoln thanked his secretary of war and enjoined everyone present to "deliberate on this matter carefully," but he also went on to warn: "We can't take to running state governments in all of these southern states. Their people must do that, although I reckon at first, they may do it badly."

Navy secretary Welles—"my Neptune," Lincoln affectionately called him—agreed that the state governments should be representative of the people's will, yet the people must not be permitted simply to reelect the same men who had instigated rebellion in the first place. The curly-bearded Dennison, who had a reputation for aloof snobbery, voiced his agreement to this, as did Stanton. Together, they suggested that the leaders of the rebellion should be identified by name and disenfranchised and disqualified from holding office. Removing these individuals from the mix, the people of each state could then choose whomever they wanted to govern themselves. Then, gratuitously, like a salesman who doesn't know when to stop talking, Stanton added that North Carolina and Virginia should be combined into a single state. There were no takers for this notion, however.

Periodically, the discussion was punctuated by the arrival of messengers. Hopeful, the cabinet members anticipated that each came bearing news from Sherman, but each in turn disappointed them.

When the discussion wound down for a moment, Lincoln, who had been mostly silent, suddenly resumed the narrative of his "indescribable vessel"/ "indefinite shore" dream, after which the general discussion shifted to the leaders of the Confederacy and what should be done with—or to—them.

Stanton, always the least charitable and the most irritable, said they should be treated as traitors, period.

Perhaps noting Lincoln's expression of obvious displeasure at this, Postmaster General Dennison offered, "I suppose, Mr. President, that you would not be sorry to have them escape out of the country?"

"I should not be sorry to see them out of the country; but I should be for following them up pretty close to make sure of their going," Lincoln replied.

One of the cabinet members pointed out that a high member of the Confederate government, Jacob Thompson, was at this very moment in Maine preparing to take ship for England.

This news reminded Lincoln of a story: "There was an Irish soldier here last summer, who wanted something to drink stronger than water. He stopped at a drug shop where he spied a soda fountain. 'Give me plase a glass of soda water, an' if yez can put in a few drops of whiskey unbeknown to anyone, I'll be obliged.'" The president paused, then continued: "Now, if Jake Thompson is permitted to go through Maine unbeknown to anyone, what's the harm?"

Now it was Stanton's countenance that betrayed displeasure, and the discussion turned to what the House and Senate would want done with the leaders of the rebellion.

"I think it is providential," Lincoln observed, "that this great rebellion is crushed just as Congress has adjourned, and there are none of the disturbing elements of that body to hinder and embarrass us. If we are wise and discreet we shall reanimate the states and get their governments in successful operation, with order prevailing and the Union reestablished before Congress comes together in December." He continued: "I hope that there will be no persecution, no bloody work after the war is over. No one need expect me to take any part in hanging or killing these men, even the worst of them. Frighten them out of the country, open the gates, let down the bars, scare them off, enough lives have been sacrificed."

Humorless, abrasive, ambitious, and arrogant, Edwin P. Stanton was also a highly capable secretary of war, and Lincoln respected him deeply. It was Stanton who uttered the first words after the president was pronounced dead: "Now he belongs to the ages."

CARRIAGE

B y two o'clock, when the cabinet meeting came to an end, the morning mists were quite gone, and the sun, no longer a ghost, had become its bright golden self. General Grant lingered behind as Lincoln's secretaries began filing out of the Cabinet Room. It is not clear just when in the day Mary Lincoln's invitation to an evening at Ford's Theatre had reached Julia Grant, but she recalled: "As soon as I received the invitation to go with Mrs. Lincoln, I dispatched a note to General Grant entreating him to go home that evening; that I did not want to go to the theater." After receiving this note, the general apparently temporized, explaining to Lincoln, presumably through a messenger, that he and his wife wanted to leave Washington this evening to visit their children at school in Burlington, New Jersey. He had a great deal of paperwork to attend to, he explained. If he could finish it tonight, he wanted to catch a train. If it was clear that he could not finish it, he would be delighted to go to the theater. Now, as he spoke with the president after the cabinet meeting, he told him that it was certain he would finish the work and that he and Mrs. Grant therefore would be off to New Jersey and unable to accompany the Lincolns. The president replied that he understood.

A few historians have reported that Secretary of War Stanton, overhearing this exchange between Lincoln and Grant, warned: "Neither of you should go to the theater tonight." While it is true that Stanton repeatedly counseled the president to avoid exposing himself to danger by venturing out after dark, especially to the theater, there is no record of his having spoken up at this time. It is also true that Stanton himself declined an invitation to attend the performance of *Our American Cousin* this evening, but that was to be expected. As opposed to Lincoln, Edwin Stanton had no appetite for the theater, which did not sit well with his straitlaced fundamentalist religious beliefs.

Tradition holds that Julia Grant begged off the invitation because she felt acutely uneasy in the company of Mary Lincoln, who was given to embarrassing outbursts, especially when she saw her husband speaking with other women. It is true that Mrs. Grant had witnessed two such incidents, and it is highly likely that she had little enough enthusiasm for spending an evening with the president's difficult wife; however, the overriding reason for declining the invitation on April 14 was certainly the Grants' eagerness to visit with their children.

Regardless of the general's reason for turning Lincoln down, a number of historians have speculated that, had he been at the theater, Booth would not have been able to get to the president. Grant, they point out, would have been accompanied by a full-dress military escort, who would have guarded not only him but the president as well. While seemingly a logical assumption, it is almost certainly unwarranted. On February 10, 1865, Grant and Lincoln went to Ford's Theatre to see John Sleeper Clarke—Booth's brother-in-law—in a double bill featuring a pair of farces, *Everybody's Friend* and *Love in Livery*. They were accompanied by Major General Ambrose Burnside, but they had neither military escort nor guards. Indeed, Abraham Lincoln was always adamant about refusing any extra guards or escorts when he attended the theater because he felt that they would interfere with the enjoyment of other playgoers.

Following the cabinet meeting, Lincoln returned to his office, where he met with three Marylanders, Governor Thomas Swann, Senator John A. J. Creswell, and Edwin H. Webster. At Lincoln's request, Swann and Creswell had brought a list of ten nominees for a variety of state offices that required the president's approval. Webster, one the nominees, had additional business: a request that Lincoln grant a pardon to a Confederate prisoner, George S. Herron, the brother of a prominent Baltimore clergyman. Incarcerated at Camp Chase, Ohio, Herron was suffering from dysentery and his brother was anxious to get him out. Lincoln accepted the offered petition, turned it over, and wrote across the back: "Let this prisoner be discharged on taking the [loyalty] oath of Dec. 8, 1863. A. Lincoln." Creswell also had a pardon request, presented on behalf of one Benjamin F. Twilley, housed in a camp at Point Lookout in St. Mary's County, Maryland. Creswell presented Lincoln with the prisoner's amnesty request, on which Creswell had written: "I respectfully ask that the within named Benjn F. Twilley be discharged on the usual terms." Lincoln added his endorsement—"Let it be done. A. Lincoln April 14, 1865"—and handed it back to Creswell.

These were only two of many pardons Lincoln signed in the waning days of the war, and there were several more on this, the fourteenth of April, including one that set free a young Confederate soldier about to be executed. "I think this boy can do more good above ground than under ground," Lincoln remarked to his secretary, John Hay. The president not only pardoned Confederate prisoners of war but also extended his mercy to many Union soldiers as well. He wrote a note to Major General George Meade, commanding the Army of the Potomac: "I am appealed to in behalf of August Bittersdorf, at Mitchells Station, Va. to be shot to-morrow as a deserter. I am unwilling for any boy under eighteen to be shot; and his father affirms that he is under sixteen. Please answer. His Regt. or Co. not given me. A. Lincoln." With so many boys dead on the battlefields of the war, Lincoln could not bear to see them killed in the name of military discipline. Once, after granting a pardon, he remarked to Schuyler Colfax: "Some of my generals complain that I impair discipline by my frequent pardons and reprieves; but it rests me after a hard day's work that I can find some excuse for saving some poor fellow's life, and I shall go to bed happy tonight as I think how joyous the signing of this name will make himself, his family and friends."

During the Civil War, Abraham Lincoln pardoned at least 760 prisoners of war, Union inmates, and condemned men. In addition to Herron, Twilley, and Bittersdorf, two more individuals, Bradford Hambrick and Patrick Murphy, received presidential pardons on April 14, 1865. An Alabama man, Hambrick was accused of intimidating loyal citizens into joining the Confederate army; he had been fined $2,000 and sentenced to a year in prison for having threatened to shoot one loyalist's wife and having attempted to hang a man. Hambrick appealed to Lincoln, who returned his letter with an endorsement: "Pardoned. A. Lincoln April 14, 1865." Murphy was a Union soldier who deserted from one regiment only to enlist in another. Although illegal, this was not an uncommon practice during the war. But Patrick Murphy was treated with exceptional harshness; found guilty of desertion, he was sentenced to be shot. Because Lincoln demanded that he be given all capital sentences to review, the Murphy case came before him. Citing a notation in Murphy's documents that the prisoner was "not perfectly sound," Lincoln returned the file with his order: "This man is pardoned and hereby discharged from the service. A. Lincoln April 14, 1865."

At some time earlier in the day—perhaps at breakfast—the president had promised Mrs. Lincoln that he would join her for a carriage ride at three that afternoon. She was particularly delighted because he had made a point of asking her not to invite anyone else: "I prefer to ride by ourselves today." As the appointed hour approached, Lincoln rose from his desk, removed his coat, rolled up his shirt sleeves, and stepped into a closet furnished with a washstand to rinse his hands. Charles A. Dana, assistant secretary of war, interrupted his ablutions with an urgent dispatch from the provost marshal at Portland, Maine. It concerned Jacob Thompson, the Confederate agent who had been mentioned in the cabinet meeting. Thompson was indeed about to arrive in Portland, where he certainly intended to board a Canadian steamer bound for Liverpool, England. After reading the dispatch aloud, Dana asked Lincoln for his orders. What did Stanton want to do? the president asked. Arrest him, Dana replied. Lincoln turned to the young man: "I rather guess not. When you have an elephant in hand, and he wants to run away, you better let him run." (In the wee hours of the morning of April 15, with Lincoln comatose, Stanton ordered the arrest of Thompson—and every other agent associated with his Canadian-based operation.)

Although they were alone together in the carriage—the driver, either Francis Burns or Ned Burke, was perched outside above them—President and Mrs. Lincoln were escorted by a small detachment of cavalry, a measure taken less out of concern over assassins and more to keep the couple from being mobbed by exuberant citizens. Presumably they drove around the city before arriving at one of the Lincolns' favorite spots, the Navy Yard, in the southeast quadrant of the capital. Mary Lincoln had a good friend in Mrs. Gustavus Fox, wife of the commandant, and relished visiting with her. As for the president, he was fascinated by ships and by great naval guns, and, in the course of the war, visited the yard at least sixty times. On this day, the couple toured USS *Montauk*, a 1,335-ton *Passaic*-class monitor commissioned in 1862. (Just three days later, on April 18, *Montauk* would serve as a prison ship, housing several of the people accused of having conspired to murder Abraham Lincoln, and, before the end of the month, on April 27, it would serve as the venue for the identification and subsequent autopsy of the body of John Wilkes Booth.)

In a marriage often steeped in gloom and punctuated by stormy emotions, this carriage ride represented one of the good times. "He was almost boyish, in his mirth," Mary Lincoln

WILLIE LINCOLN, THIRD SON OF PRESIDENT LINCOLN,
DIED FEBRUARY 20, 1862, AT THE AGE OF 12.
From a photograph taken by Brady at Washington, shortly
before the death of Willie Lincoln.

Willie Lincoln, third son of Mary and Abraham, died in the White House on
February 20, 1862. He was twelve years old.

wrote in a letter more than half a year later, "& reminded me, of his original nature, what I had always remembered of him, in our own home—free from care, . . . I never saw him so supremely cheerful—his manner was even playful. . . . During the drive he was so gay, that I said to him, laughingly, 'Dear Husband, you almost startle me by your great cheerfulness,' he replied, 'and well I may feel so, Mary, I consider *this day*, the war has come to a close.'" But then, characteristically, a note of melancholy intruded: "We must both," he said, "be more cheerful in the future—between the war and the loss of our darling Willie—we have both, been very miserable."

DUSK

S hortly after five, the Lincolns' carriage rolled up the White House drive, just in time for the president to catch sight of two friends, who, having discovered Lincoln absent when they came to call, were just leaving. Recognizing Illinois governor Richard Oglesby and politician turned brigadier general Isham Haynie, Lincoln called to them from the carriage and invited them into the White House, where he promptly began reading to them aloud. The president loved to read aloud, especially favorite passages of humor and political satire. Much to the consternation of no-nonsense members like war secretary Edwin Stanton and stuffed shirts like Postmaster General Dennison, he even did this routinely during cabinet meetings. According to Edward Steers, Jr., the most reliable modern authority on the Lincoln assassination, Lincoln read to Oglesby and Haynie from *Phoenixiana; or, Sketches and Burlesques*, a collection of political satires by George H. Derby, who wrote under the pen names of John Phoenix and, sometimes, Squibob. Others believe that, on this occasion, he shared favorite passages from *The Nasby Papers*, by David Ross Locke, who satirized the Confederate cause throughout the war in a series of newspaper articles written in a coarsely comic Southern dialect under the name of Petroleum V. Nasby. The middle initial stood for "Vesuvius," and it reflected the explosive bombast of Locke's comically quasi-literate secessionist persona. Still others hold that Lincoln did not read from the Nasby book but from Nasby columns freshly clipped from recent newspapers. Lincoln was well known to relish these columns, reading them at night in bed, often moved to laughter so hard that he cried, as he peered out his bedroom door in search of someone with whom to share an especially delectable passage.

Whatever Abraham Lincoln read to Governor Oglesby and Brigadier General Haynie, he took so much delight in it that he repeatedly put off the White House butler's call to dinner. According to one of Mary Lincoln's biographers, the president "promised . . . to go" after each call "but would continue reading the book. Finally, he received a peremptory order from the butler that he must come to dinner at once." The president invited the two men to join him and his family, but they both pleaded prior engagements and promised to call again during the weekend.

Dinner lasted from 7:00 to 7:30, abbreviated, doubtless, so that the Lincolns could make an eight o'clock curtain at Ford's. Steers believes that the president and his wife ate alone, but others have reported that the couple dined with Tad and Robert, who took the opportunity to remind his mother that he was going out with friends and that he wasn't certain he'd be able to make use of the Grover's Theatre tickets she had given him. At least one chronicler of Lincoln's final day, Jim Bishop, believes that this prompted Mrs. Lincoln to announce at table that she had invited Major Henry Rathbone and his fiancée, Clara Harris, to replace the Grants as their companions for the evening. (Actually, the couple was Mary Lincoln's *third* choice, after the Grants, and after Major Thomas Eckert, assistant secretary of war, who had pleaded an excess of work that evening.) Following the death of his father, Henry Rathbone's mother had married New York senator Ira Harris, a widower, among whose children was a lively brunet daughter, Clara. In 1865, Henry Rathbone became engaged to his stepsister.

Time was awasting, and the Lincolns would have to pick up the major and his lady en route to the theater.

LATECOMERS

espite the ticking clock, Abraham Lincoln saw at least one other visitor before leaving for the theater. Speaker of the House Schuyler Colfax, with whom he had met in the morning, had some last-minute matters to discuss before he was to leave for California on the fifteenth. In the course of this meeting, Lincoln mentioned to Colfax that Senator Charles Sumner had, after the fall of Richmond, obtained the gavel of the Confederate Congress. Sumner intended to present it to Stanton, but Lincoln asked him to give it instead to the Speaker, the more appropriate recipient.

According to *Through Five Administrations*, a memoir published in 1907 by William Crook, one of the president's bodyguards, Lincoln had yet another meeting before leaving for Ford's. Crook was responsible for the 8 A.M. to 4 P.M. shift, but when his relief, Officer John F. Parker, failed to show up, Crook remained on duty. In his memoir, Crook wrote that after the president's dinner, he accompanied Lincoln to the War Department, which was housed on the White House grounds along 17th Street. Crook wrote that Lincoln seemed profoundly depressed, and when the pair passed a group of apparent drunkards

Lincoln remarked: "Crook, do you know I believe there are men who want to take my life? And I have no doubt, they will do it." Startled by the remark, Crook asked Lincoln why he thought this. "Other men have been assassinated," he replied. "I know no one could do it and escape alive. But if it is to be done, it is impossible to prevent." Crook wrote that Lincoln had no desire to go to the theater that night, but had yielded to Mrs. Lincoln's insistence. After his brief meeting with Stanton, the president parted from his bodyguard. Instead of his customary "Good night," he said, ominously, "Good-bye, Crook."

The dramatic poignancy of William Crook's recollection has appealed to almost every writer who has told the story of Lincoln's last Good Friday. However, Edward Steers, Jr., makes a good argument that Crook either misremembered the events of April 14 or deliberately fabricated a touching story. To begin with, the president's visit with Schuyler Colfax conflicts with the timeline of Crook's narrative; moreover, the historical record seems to indicate that the meeting with Stanton had taken place two days earlier, on April 12. Indeed, Steers believes that Parker had actually relieved Crook on schedule, and that Crook was not even present in the White House after 4 P.M.

If Crook's memoir was mistaken or blatantly false, the greatest disservice was done to Mary Lincoln, whom Crook (and, after him, many others as well) blamed for effectively leading her husband to his death. As already noted, Lincoln delighted in the theater, and, some two months after the assassination, Mary wrote to Francis Carpenter (a New York painter who had lived in the White House for six months in 1864 and painted *First Reading of the Emancipation Proclamation by President Lincoln*, a well-known tableau, as well as a family portrait of the Lincolns) that she had a bad headache and wanted to stay home on the evening of April 14 but that her husband's "mind . . . was fixed upon having some relaxation & bent on the theater." It was *she* who did not want to disappoint *him*.

The truth seems to be that Lincoln and Colfax talked until 8 P.M.—curtain time—and that he did not meet with Stanton; however, two more callers were waiting, Massachusetts congressman George Ashmun and his friend Judge Charles P. Daly. Lincoln withdrew a card from his pocket and wrote: "Allow Mr. Ashmun & friend to come in at 9 A.M. to-morrow. A. Lincoln." These were the last words the president wrote.

Abraham and Mary Lincoln climbed into their carriage shortly after eight. With them was driver Ned Burke and valet Charles Forbes. The president's standing order was that no cavalry escort was to accompany him and his wife either to church or to the theater. They drove off, stopping first at the Harris residence, at 15th and H Streets, just across from the White House, where they picked up Henry Rathbone and his fiancée C lara Harris. There were strict regulations governing the presence and activity of soldiers within the city limits of wartime Washington, D.C., so many officers who were off-duty took to wearing civilian clothing. Major Rathbone was not in uniform, and he was unarmed.

The carriage reached the theater door at 8:25. Forbes alighted first to assist the Lincolns, Rathbone, and Harris as they exited. Metropolitan Police officer John F. Parker, the president's regular evening-shift bodyguard, had arrived in advance to inspect the theater and the State Box, which was actually boxes 7 and 8 with the thin pine partition normally separating them removed. Finding all in order, he went out to the front door to await the arrival of the presidential party.

Assuming that Parker had even noticed, he neither reported nor apparently worried that the lock on the door to box 7 was broken. On March 7, Ford's Theatre ticket seller Thomas Raybold sold four orchestra seats to Thomas Merrick. Merrick and his party arrived late, however, and discovered that their seats had been taken. Embarrassed, Raybold offered to show Merrick and his guests to the best available seats and took them to box 6, only to discover that it was locked. The keys, unfortunately, were unavailable because Mr. Ford had given them to the usher, who was home ill. Why keep the boxes locked? If they were left open, the stage hands had a disagreeable habit of sleeping in them, and Mr. Ford didn't like that.

Thomas Raybold led his increasingly disgruntled patrons to box 7, which was also locked, and then to box 8. Finding it locked as well, he shouldered the door. Hard. When this failed to budge it, Raybold returned to box 7 and, releasing his pent-up frustration, kicked the lock and broke it. He apologetically seated his guests, but he never reported the damage to the lock, and it was still broken on April 14.

With John Parker taking the lead and Charles Forbes, carrying Lincoln's favorite plaid shawl (the president often complained of chill), bringing up the rear, the presidential party made its way into the theater, up the stairs to the balcony, crossing over to the State Box along the south wall of the theater. Patrons in the first balcony—the "dress circle"—seeing

68

the president's arrival, rose and applauded. On stage, Laura Keene (playing Florence Trenchard) was trading puns with the resolutely clueless Lord Dundreary. They bantered about a window *draft*, a *draught* of medicine, and a bank *draft*.

"Good gracious!" Keene's character exclaimed. "You have almost a game of *draughts*."

This sent Dundreary into a convulsion of stage laughter.

"What is the matter?" asked Keene.

"That wath a joke," Dundreary sputtered, "that wath."

Now seeing the president and party making their way to the box, Laura Keene stepped out of character, stopped the action, looked to the guests of honor, and joined the swelling applause. At this, the entire theater, some 1,675 patrons, rose to its feet and applauded.

With quick wit, Laura Keene ad libbed yet another pun—"The draft has been suspended"—and the orchestra leader, Professor W. Withers, Jr., raised his baton to strike up "Hail to the Chief." By the time the tune had ended, the presidential party was seated and the valet Forbes offered the president his shawl, which he declined for now. Officer Parker sat on a cane chair placed outside the outer door, his back to the small blind corridor behind the adjoining boxes 7 and 8. He would not sit here for long, however.

Comfortably settled in the high-backed rocker that was positioned for him toward the rear of box 7, the president was soon attending to the play, but he was not so engrossed that he failed to notice how Major Rathbone had taken Clara Harris's hand in his. Lincoln took his wife's hand.

"What will Miss Harris think of my hanging on to you so?"

"Why, she will think nothing about it," Abraham Lincoln replied.

Longtime senator from Massachusetts (1852–1874), Charles Sumner was a vigorous abolitionist whose denunciation of the Kansas-Nebraska Act in 1856 as "in every respect a swindle" provoked a brutal caning on the Senate floor by Congressman Preston S. Brooks of South Carolina. It took Sumner three years to recover from the beating. A loyal supporter of Lincoln, Sumner was present at his deathbed and put a comforting arm around young Robert Lincoln.

The management of Ford's Theatre saw to it that Lincoln's box was furnished with a comfortable rocking chair the president favored. He was shot to death while sitting in it.

BOOTH

J ohn Wilkes Booth has been called a madman, a drunkard, and a failed actor. In truth, he was none of these. Although he was bigoted, bombastic, and highly emotional, no one who actually knew him thought him mad. Although he drank, no one who knew him thought he was a drunk. Born in 1838, the ninth of actor Junius Brutus Booth's ten children, John Wilkes never attracted the acclaim enjoyed by his brother Edwin, regarded as the greatest actor of his day, but he was hardly a failure. For his work on stage, John Wilkes Booth regularly earned $20,000 a year in an age when a common laborer eked out about a dollar a day.

Maryland, the state of Booth's birth and upbringing, did not secede from the Union during the Civil War, but some of its citizens held slaves, and many—probably most— identified more closely with the South than with the North. As for John Wilkes Booth, it was always audiences in the deep South who liked him best, and that fact probably helped make him a passionate supporter of the Confederacy, an advocate of slavery, and a hater of the man Southerners called "Black Lincoln." On December 2, 1859, as a volunteer

Popular legend often portrays John Wilkes Booth as a "failed" actor. In fact, he was highly popular right up to the very night he murdered Abraham Lincoln. An avid theatergoer, the president had even seen him perform at least once, on November 9, 1863, in Charles Selby's *The Marble Heart*, a play about Raphael, in which Booth portrayed the artist. Booth is pictured here, at the height of his success.

serving with the Richmond militia, Booth was present at the hanging of the militant abolitionist John Brown, but, once the Civil War actually began, Booth did not take up arms on behalf of the Confederacy. Still, during the war years, he talked loudly and frequently about "the Cause," and he befriended a number of men known to be active in the so-called Confederate "secret service," spies and couriers. Booth may even have undertaken espionage or courier missions himself. The very fact that the face of the darkly handsome Booth was so well known—dashingly trimmed handlebar moustache, spit curls set meticulously against his broad forehead—helped place him above suspicion. He could hide in plain sight.

Speculation and debate over Booth's relation to the Confederate government began from the very moment his name was connected with the events of April 14, 1865. Secretary of War Edwin Stanton immediately concluded he was an agent of the Confederacy, but most later historians have assumed he and his handful of conspirators were acting on their own. Beginning in the fall of 1864, Booth hatched a series of bizarre plots to kidnap Lincoln and exchange him for Confederate prisoners of war. During this period, he wrote a letter justifying the planned kidnapping and entrusted it, sealed, to his sister's husband, the actor John Sleeper Clarke. The letter was signed, "A Confederate doing duty upon his own responsibility. J. Wilkes Booth," something that has lent credibility to those who believe Booth operated on his own. Yet broader conspiracy theories have never been put to rest, including claims that Vice President Andrew Johnson was involved with Booth, that Secretary of War Edwin Stanton was the mastermind of the assassination, that international bankers were behind it, that it was a plot of the Catholic Church, or that Booth was, in fact, an agent of the Confederacy and that Confederate secretary of state Judah P. Benjamin was pulling the strings.

Of all the conspiracy theories, those depicting John Wilkes Booth as a Confederate agent are the most plausible. But even if the Confederate government was behind a kidnapping scheme or even an assassination plot, Booth himself commanded nothing more than a pathetic little band of misfit conspirators. After the abduction plots fizzled through the winter of 1864–1865, Booth was left with just three men in April 1865 when he suddenly abandoned the notion of abduction altogether (it made no sense with the war all but finally lost) and embraced assassination instead. George A. Atzerodt was a dipsomaniac Maryland carriage maker. David Herold was a drugstore clerk, aged twenty-three, who had an infantile intellect and a puppylike desire to please Booth. Added to this pair was a large, square, powerfully built former Confederate soldier who called himself Lewis "Payne" Paine, but whose real name was Lewis Thornton Powell.

As a prominent actor, John Wilkes Booth was well known at both Grover's Theatre and at Ford's. By talking with his friends in theater management, he learned that the Lincolns had tickets to Grover's on April 14 but that they had decided to go to Ford's instead—and that General Grant would be with them. He decided to kill both Lincoln and Grant while Atzerodt would kill Andrew Johnson and Paine and Herold would murder the injured secretary of state William H. Seward.

Booth knew the layout of Ford's Theatre well, but during

To George A. Atzerodt, an alcoholic carriage maker from Maryland, John Wilkes Booth assigned the task of assassinating Vice President Andrew Johnson. Atzerodt never even made the attempt. Nevertheless, he was caught, tried, and hanged.

John Wilkes Booth used this gun to assassinate President Lincoln. Manufactured in Philadelphia by John Deringer, the weapon is most properly described as "a cap-and-ball pocket pistol." The Deringer firm specialized in such diminutive firearms, which were popularly called derringers (usually spelled with two r's). The term was soon applied generically to any small pistol by any maker.

the day on April 14 he inspected the State Box very carefully. An outer door opened onto a small blind corridor, along which were the doors to box 7 and box 8, which, with their partition removed, were combined into a single box. Booth noted that the lock on the door to box 7 was broken. He also noted that a small hole had been drilled into that door. For years after the assassination, it was assumed that Booth had drilled the hole in preparation for his infamous deed; however, in 1962, Frank Ford, son of Harry Clay Ford, one of the theater's owners, revealed that the hole had been made on the orders of his father, so that Lincoln's guard could look into the box without having to disturb the occupants by repeatedly opening the door. Finally, Booth also obtained a piece of wood from a music stand backstage, which he planned to use to wedge the outer door shut behind him while he killed Lincoln and Grant.

For so momentous a mission, John Wilkes Booth armed himself lightly, with just a bowie knife and a diminutive single-shot derringer. He planned to use the knife on Lincoln's guard, then on the president, reserving the derringer for Grant. With the outer door wedged shut, he would then leap over the railing of the box, onto the stage, cross the stage to the north wing, make his way through the backstage area, then exit through the rear of the theater, to a driveway called "Baptist Alley," where he had a horse waiting for him.

In the course of the day of April 14, Booth learned that General Grant would not be with Lincoln after all. His only target would be the president, and he would therefore use the derringer on him. Because he was thoroughly familiar with the script of *Our American Cousin*, Booth was able to choose the very moment to fire his single shot. There was a line that always drew the biggest laugh in the play. The pretentious English mother, Mrs. Mountchessington, declares to Harry Hawk's character, Asa Trenchard, "I am aware, Mr. Trenchard, that you are not used to the manners of good society, and that alone will excuse the impertinence of which you have been guilty." Trenchard, the backwoods American, drawls in reply, "Don't know the manners of good society, eh? Well, I guess I know enough to turn you inside out, old gal—you sockdologizing old mantrap," and the audience erupts into

David E. Herold, a twenty-three-year-old drugstore clerk who followed John Wilkes Booth like a faithful puppy, was assigned to hold the getaway horse while Lewis Paine murdered Secretary of State William Seward.

laughter. They always did. Booth calculated that this line would be delivered about 10:15 P.M.

Despite John Wilkes Booth's planning, things went wrong from the start. George Atzerodt got cold feet and never even attempted to kill Vice President Johnson. David Herold held Lewis Paine's horse while the latter proceeded to make a bloody mess of the Seward assassination. In the course of the attempt on the secretary of state's life, Paine fractured the skull of Seward's son, Assistant Secretary of State Frederick Seward, slashed the forehead of a male military nurse named George T. Robinson, knocked unconscious Seward's young daughter, Fanny, then stabbed Seward himself repeatedly, tearing a gaping hole in his cheek before Seward saved himself by rolling off and under the bed. In the meantime, Robinson revived sufficiently to attack Paine, who then stabbed Robinson as another of Seward's sons, Major Augustus Seward, entered the bedroom and was slashed on the forehead and hand. Paine ran out of the bedroom and down the stairs, where he encountered a State Department messenger, whom he slashed. Running out the front door of the Seward house, Paine screamed, "I am mad! I am mad!" (Mayhem notwithstanding, all survived and recovered from the assassination attempt.)

Just as Lewis Paine was beginning his bloody evening's work, John Wilkes Booth calmly made his way to the State Box. He approached the outer door, prepared to dispatch the president's bodyguard with his bowie knife. But Officer John F. Parker was not at his assigned post in front of the outer door to boxes 7 and 8. Tradition has it that Parker, having become bored with sitting outside the box, his back to the stage, nipped into Taltavul's Saloon, next door to the theater, for a drink. This may have been the case, but there is no hard evidence. The only thing certain is that Parker, for whatever reason, was not at his post when Booth approached, then entered the blind corridor, wedged closed the outer door, and peered through the convenient hole in the door to box 7.

He saw the presidential rocker, the head resting against the chair's high back. At about 10:15, as Harry Hawk delivered the anticipated line and the audience, as anticipated, erupted in laughter, Booth gingerly opened the door, entered the box, leveled his derringer between Lincoln's left ear and spine, and from a distance of no more than twenty-four inches squeezed the trigger and discharged the weapon's half-inch-diameter ball.

Propelled by the derringer's light charge, the projectile entered Abraham Lincoln's skull at its base, traveled through the brain diagonally from left to right, and came to violent rest behind the right eye, fracturing the orbital socket. Nobody—except for Booth—witnessed the immediate effect on the president, but, doubtless, he slumped instantly in his chair, his chin falling against his chest.

In timing his shot, John Wilkes Booth had planned well indeed. Perhaps no one in the audience heard the report of the diminutive weapon. Even Mrs. Lincoln, seated next to her husband, Rathbone, and Clara Harris were hardly startled by the dull pop. But very soon a blue cloud of smoke drifted above the balcony and over the stage. A scream shrilled from the State Box, then the sounds of a scuffle as Major Rathbone tangled with Booth, who, stabbing him in the arm and tearing a deep

America's leading popular image maker, Currier and Ives, published this depiction of the assassination.

gash that ran from shoulder to elbow, broke free. Booth swung his legs over the balustrade, which was festooned with a pair of flags—the banner of the Treasury Regiment on box 7 and the Stars and Stripes on box 8. Booth, dressed in a stylish black suit, his tightly tailored trousers stuffed into highly polished tan calf-length boots, caught his right spur in the Treasury Regiment flag, which, as he leaped to the stage below, caused his left foot to absorb the full weight of his fall. The small bone in that leg snapped on impact a few inches above the ankle.

As a dazed Harry Hawk stood frozen center stage, Booth

raised himself from a crouch, theatrically thrust his arms into the air, and shouted: "*Sic semper tyrannis!*" The state motto of Virginia, it translates: "Thus always to tyrants."

Now the shouting began. "Stop that man!" "It's Booth!" "Stop that man!" But in the confusion, no one did, and John Wilkes Booth lurched across the stage, just as he had planned, made his way backstage and opened the door onto Baptist Alley. His waiting horse was being held by a young peanut vendor and Ford's Theatre factotum named Johnny "Peanuts" Burroughs. He lay on a carpenter's bench as he held the reins. Booth struck him hard on the head with the handle of his bowie knife, seized the reins from him, and rode off. No one gave chase.

DEATH WATCH

Except for Henry Rathbone, who had grappled with Booth, twenty-three-year-old army surgeon Charles Augustus Leale was the first person in the audience of 1,675 to come to the stricken president's aid. Like Rathbone, Leale was dressed in civilian clothes to avoid being harassed by provost police enforcing strict regulations governing the presence of men in uniform in the capital. He had little enough interest in *Our American Cousin*, but he had boundless admiration for Abraham Lincoln and had attended the theater hoping to steal a glimpse of his hero. He had been seated in the dress circle, not far from the State Box. Plowing his way through the crowd, he reached the outer door of the box, but because of the piece of wood Booth had positioned behind it Leale was unable to force the door. Indeed, the harder he pushed, the more tightly it became wedged, even as the wounded Rathbone, unbeknownst to Leale, struggled to remove the wood. Leale stepped back a moment to get a fresh angle on the door, whereupon Rathbone was finally able to free it. Presidential valet Charles Forbes stood in the doorway but yielded when Leale identified himself as a surgeon. Soon, Dr. Albert F. A. King, an army physician, and

Dr. Charles Augustus Leale, a twenty-three-year-old army surgeon, was the first person in the Ford's Theatre audience to come to the wounded president's aid. He is shown here in the double image of a stereopticon photograph.

government employee William Kent followed Leale into the box.

Rathbone, badly bleeding, asked Leale to attend to his torn arm, but the physician turned to the president first. In contrast to Rathbone, whose blood "saturated" his fiancé's clothing, Lincoln hardly bled, and Leale was hard pressed to locate the site of the injury, as Mary Lincoln held her husband upright to keep him from falling forward and out of the rocker. "As I looked at Lincoln he appeared dead. His eyes were closed and his head had fallen forward." Finding no pulse, Leale and others gently laid Lincoln on the floor, Leale supporting the president's head. The surgeon's hand came away slightly bloody. His first thought was that the president had been stabbed in the back or the neck.

At this point, audience member Thomas Bradford Sanders boosted Dr. Charles Sabin Taft, another army surgeon, from the orchestra level up over the balustrade and into the president's box. Behind him was Lieutenant James Bolton of the D.C. provost marshal's guard. Although senior in rank to Leale, Taft deferred to the younger doctor and assisted him in looking for the site of the president's wound. Leale borrowed a penknife to cut away Lincoln's collar and split open his shirt and coat.

The doctors looked and felt. No wound.

Leale lifted Lincoln's eyelids. Noting that the pupil of the left eye was fixed and dilated, he quickly concluded that there was neurological damage. He ran his fingers through Lincoln's hair and discovered the entry wound at the back of the head. It was clotted. The surgeon removed the clot, and the comatose president, who had been struggling for breath, began to breathe more easily.

At some point, Leale turned to Taft: "I can't save him. His

wound is mortal. It is impossible for him to recover." His eyes welled up with tears.

At some point, too, yet another person crowded into the State Box. It was Laura Keene. Standing in the wings, stunned like everyone else, she had responded to a call for water, and, grabbing a pitcher from the green room, made her way up a set of back stairs to the box. "While we were waiting for Mr. Lincoln to regain strength," Leale later recalled, "Laura Keene appealed to me to allow her to hold the President's head. I granted the request, and she sat on the floor of the box and held his head in her lap." (She would preserve the dress stained with Lincoln's blood for the rest of her life.)

Discussion now turned to whether the president should be moved to the White House. Charles Leale and the two other doctors agreed that the seven-block trip would probably kill him. When someone ran next door to inquire if Lincoln might be brought to Taltavul's Saloon, Mr. Taltavul replied that it "would not be right" for the president to die in a saloon. Leale decided that his patient should be taken to the nearest available house across the street, and he assigned Dr. Taft to carry his right shoulder, Dr. King his left, and "a sufficient number of others"— four soldiers from Thompson's Battery C, Independent Pennsylvania Artillery—"to assist in carrying the body, while I carried the head going first."

Dr. Leale's patient was carried down the stairs and into the lobby, where two more soldiers, William McPeck and John Weaver, assisted in bearing the wounded man. Outside, ten members of the Union Light Guard quickly formed a human corridor to the street.

Now the bearers scanned 10th Street for a suitable,

The stricken president was taken to this bedroom in the house of William Petersen, across the street from Ford's Theatre. He lay on this bed through the night of April 14 and died upon it at twenty-two minutes and ten seconds after seven o'clock the following morning.

available house. Suddenly, a young man, Henry S. Safford, candle in hand, appeared at the front door of the house of William Petersen, tailor, at 453 (now 516) 10th Street, diagonally across from the main entrance to Ford's Theatre.

"Bring him in here! Bring him in here!" he shouted, lifting the candle.

Safford, one of nine paying boarders who lived with the nine-member Petersen family, led the way to a nine-and-a-half-by-seventeen-foot bedroom, furnished with a bed, a dresser and two chairs. It was much too short for Lincoln, but removing the footboard was quickly rejected because it would cause the bed to collapse. Instead, the president was laid diagonally across the bed, which was moved out from the wall so that the doctors could more easily attend to their patient.

As the doctors prepared to remove the rest of Lincoln's clothes so that they could examine him more thoroughly, Mrs. Lincoln and others were ushered into the front parlor of the house. The physicians found no additional injuries, but, noting that the president's hands and feet were ice cold, Dr. Leale ordered hot-water bottles, warm blankets, and a mustard plaster for Lincoln's chest. After completing their examination, and having arranged the bedcovers over the president, the doctors summoned Mrs. Lincoln, who sat by her husband's head, kissing him and imploring him to say just one word to her.

Within a short time, Robert Lincoln was summoned to join the vigil at the Petersen house. He brought with him Elizabeth Dixon, wife of Senator James Dixon of Connecticut, and she stayed by Mary Lincoln's side throughout the long night, gently leading her out of the bedroom when her cries and

In the double parlor of William Petersen's house, Mary Todd Lincoln and others held vigil through the terrible night and early morning of April 14/15, 1865.

pleadings interfered with the doctors' work—work that consisted of little more than periodically removing the clot of blood that formed at the entry wound. Each time a clot was removed, Lincoln's breathing improved.

The president was doomed, of course, but when he at last appeared reasonably comfortable Dr. Leale took time out to write a note summoning Lincoln's pastor, the Reverend Phineas T. Gurley, of the New York Avenue Presbyterian Church. Leale also dispatched notes to Surgeon General Joseph K. Barnes, Dr.

Willard Bliss (Leale's commanding officer at the Armory Square Hospital), and Dr. Robert K. Stone (the Lincoln family physician). This done, he sent word to every member of the cabinet, instructing the messenger to call on Edwin Stanton first.

Before Leale's messenger reached Stanton, the secretary of war was preparing for bed. Suddenly, he was startled by a scream from his wife downstairs: "My God! Mr. Seward has been murdered!" The news had come from another messenger, who then led the secretary of war to a waiting carriage. Arriving at Seward's house, Stanton met navy secretary Gideon Welles, who had already heard about the events at Ford's Theatre and informed Stanton that Lincoln had been shot. Stanton and Welles entered the Seward house, saw the carnage, but decided that Seward might well recover and that their more immediate duty lay with the president. Against the advice of army officers concerned for their safety, the pair drove off to the Petersen house, reaching it shortly after eleven. There, after looking in on Lincoln and immediately concluding that he, unlike Seward, would definitely die, Stanton set up the government of the United States in the rear parlor, effectively appointing himself acting president in a leap over the constitutionally mandated succession (a century before the Twenty-fifth Amendment of 1967) of vice president, president pro tempore of the Senate, and Speaker of the House. His first order of business was to take testimony from witnesses and to dispatch police officers and soldiers to hunt down the guilty. Present throughout these proceedings was Corporal James Tanner, who, having lost his legs at the second Battle of Bull Run, used his long convalescence to learn the art of shorthand, or, as it was called

On the night of April 14, 1865, William Henry Seward, Lincoln's able
secretary of state, was in bed convalescing from severe injuries sustained in
a carriage accident. Miraculously, the ailing sixty-four-year old survived a
horrifically bloody assassination attempt at the hands of Lewis Paine and
went on to earn his place in history as the man who negotiated the purchase
of Alaska from the czar of Russia in 1867.

After Lincoln had been carried to the Petersen house, U.S. Army Surgeon General Joseph K. Barnes was summoned to his bedside. Twelve days after he pronounced Abraham Lincoln dead, Dr. Barnes would perform an autopsy on the body of his assassin, John Wilkes Booth.

in the 1860s, "phonography." Transcribing everything for Stanton, he later wrote that "In fifteen minutes I had testimony enough down to hang John Wilkes Booth, the assassin, higher than ever Haman hanged."

No one in the Petersen house, save Abraham Lincoln, slept that dark night and gloomy morning. Mary Lincoln alternated between the bedroom and the front parlor, sobbing without intermission. In the rear parlor, all night long and well into the morning, Stanton conducted his inquiry and

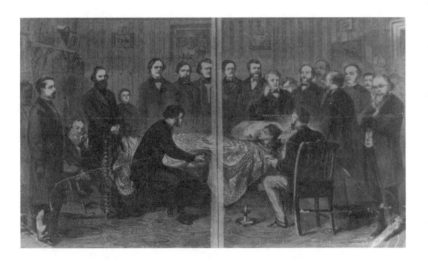

Frank Leslie's Illustrated News was a popular national weekly, which brought Americans engraved images of the Civil War before the technology to reproduced photographs in print was widely available. This depiction of "The dying moments of President Lincoln, Saturday morning, April 15" was published in the newspaper on April 29, 1865.

coordinated the manhunt.

All the while, the doctors watched their patient. Beyond periodically dislodging clots from the wound and applying more hot-water bottles, there was nothing they *could* do but watch. Shortly before seven in the morning, it became apparent that the end was now very near. Indeed, Leale and the others were surprised that the president, so gravely wounded, had lasted through the night. Mary Lincoln was summoned from the front parlor. Leale recalled the scene: "As she entered the chamber and saw how the beloved features were distorted, she fell fainting to the floor. Restoratives were applied, and she was supported to the bedside, where she frantically addressed the dying man. 'Love,' she exclaimed, 'live but one moment to speak to me once—to speak to our children.' "

Mary Lincoln was led back to the front parlor. Charles Leale sat on one side at the head of the bed, Surgeon General Barnes on the opposite side, Dr. Stone at the foot, and Robert Lincoln stood next to Senator Charles Sumner, who put his arm around him. Leale held the president's hand, his forefinger over the pulse.

Soon, there was no pulse. Then no signs of respiration, either.

Leale looked at Surgeon General Barnes. Simultaneously, the two men closed their eyes for several seconds. Barnes rose, peeled back one of Lincoln's eyelids, then put his ear to the president's chest. Through the plaster that had been applied, he listened for what seemed a very long time before tenderly crossing Abraham Lincoln's hands across his chest. Barnes said in a low whisper: "He is gone." Tradition holds that he also withdrew a pair of silver coins from his vest pocket and placed

The Reverend Phineas Densmore Gurley of the New York Avenue
Presbyterian Church was the Lincolns' pastor. Summoned to the Petersen
house, it was he who invoked the final prayer over the president's body,
asking God to accept Abraham Lincoln, His humble servant, into His
glorious Kingdom.

them on the president's eyes. It was twenty-two minutes and ten seconds after seven o'clock in the morning, April 15, 1865.

Silence consumed the next several minutes. At last, Edwin Stanton turned to Reverend Gurley: "Doctor, will you say anything?"

Nodding his assent, Gurley knelt beside the bed and remained silent as the others in the room fell to their knees. In silence still, all placed their hands on the bed. The reverend began to pray aloud, asking God to accept Abraham Lincoln, His humble servant, into His glorious Kingdom.

The physicians who attended Lincoln at Ford's Theatre did not believe he could survive even the short carriage ride back to the White House, so the president was carried across the street to the house of tailor William Petersen, at 453 (now 516) Tenth Street.

Stanton, who, with Lincoln, had directed the cruelest, costliest war the nation ever fought, cried, and through his tears uttered the words history has accepted as the epitaph of the sixteenth president: "Now he belongs to the ages."

This stereopticon image depicts the procession of Lincoln's funeral down Pennsylvania Avenue, Washington, D.C. After a period of lying in state, the president's body was transported by a solemn, slow funeral train to his hometown or Springfield, Illinois, for burial.

EPILOGUE

For eleven days after Abraham Lincoln died, John Wilkes Booth eluded the thousands of soldiers, policemen, and detectives sent in pursuit of him. After midnight, on April 26, a detachment of Union cavalry ran him to ground at Richard Garrett's tobacco farm near Port Royal, Virginia. He and David Herold huddled in a tobacco barn. Herold quickly surrendered but Booth refused. Meaning to drive him out, the troopers set the barn ablaze. Through a window, the assassin appeared, a broken-legged man leaning on a crutch, silhouetted against the flames and cradling a carbine in his free arm. Without orders to do so, Sergeant Boston Corbett fired his Colt .45 revolver once at the silhouette. The bullet passed through the actor's neck.

The troopers dragged Booth out of the blazing barn. The bullet having severed his spinal cord, the assassin was paralyzed. Everton J. Conger, an officer of a quasi-official agency dubbed the "National Detective Police," knelt to Booth and put his ear close to his lips.

"Tell . . . Mother . . . I . . . died . . . for my country," Booth gasped out.

The words, John Wilkes Booth's last, were spoken at sunup

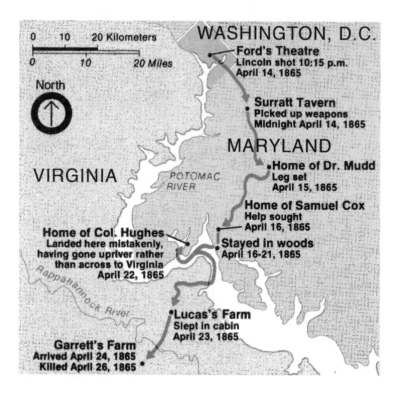

0   10   20 Kilometers

0   10   20 Miles

North

WASHINGTON, D.C.

Ford's Theatre
Lincoln shot 10:15 p.m.
April 14, 1865

Surratt Tavern
Picked up weapons
Midnight April 14, 1865

MARYLAND

Home of Dr. Mudd
Leg set
April 15, 1865

VIRGINIA

POTOMAC
RIVER

Home of Samuel Cox
Help sought
April 16, 1865

Home of Col. Hughes
Landed here mistakenly,
having gone upriver rather
than across to Virginia
April 22, 1865

Stayed in woods
April 16-21, 1865

Rappahannock River

Lucas's Farm
Slept in cabin
April 23, 1865

Garrett's Farm
Arrived April 24, 1865
Killed April 26, 1865

John Wilkes Booth easily evaded capture, even after shooting the president in a theater packed with 1,675 patrons, breaking his leg by jumping from the president's box to the stage, and pausing to declaim to the bewildered audience "Sic semper tyrannis"—the Latin motto of the state of Virginia: Thus ever to tyrants. He made his way into Maryland, stopping at the home of Dr. Samuel Mudd to have his broken leg set, then rode into Virginia, where, on April 24, he holed up at the tobacco farm of Richard Garrett a few miles below the Rappahannock River. Two days later, a detachment of U.S. cavalry troops surrounded the tobacco barn in which he and accomplice David Herold hid. Herold surrendered, Booth put up a fight, was shot, and was mortally wounded. He died on the scene.

This three-story building at 604 H Street, NW, Washington, D.C., was the boarding house owned and operated by Mary Surratt. Here John Wilkes Booth and six others, including Mary's son, John, plotted the abduction of President Lincoln and, after this abortive plot failed, his assassination. (John Surratt admitted participating in the plot of the abduction, but denied any involvement in the assassination.)

John Surratt, Jr., postmaster of Surrattsville, Maryland, served the Confederacy during the Civil War as a secret agent and courier. Through Dr. Samuel Mudd, he met John Wilkes Booth on December 23, 1864, and conspired with him and others to abduct President Lincoln during March 1865. When this miscarried, Surratt (by his own account) fled Washington and, on April 14, 1865 (he claimed), was in Elmira, New York, on an espionage mission. Taking flight to Canada after hearing of the assassination, he remained there until September, when he set sail for England. He subsequently joined the Papal Zouaves (formed in 1860 to defend the Papal States) and was sufficiently proud of his membership in this unit to have himself photographed in a Zouave uniform. While he was visiting Alexandria, Egypt, late in 1866, Surratt was identified as a Lincoln assassination conspirator, arrested, and returned to the United States for trial. This proceedings began on June 10, 1867 and ended in a hung jury on August 10. Charges were then dropped, Surratt was released, and he made a small fortune giving public lectures about his life as a Confederate spy and an intimate of Booth. He died of pneumonia in 1916.

Dr. Samuel Mudd was a slave-holding rural Maryland farmer, physician, and Confederate sympathizer. He splinted Booth's broken leg early in the assassin's eleven-day flight from justice--an act for which he was sentenced to life imprisonment. While serving his time in a military prison on the Dry Tortugas off the coast of Florida, Mudd, though sick himself, nursed guards and fellow inmates through a yellow fever epidemic. Grateful prison officials signed a petition for Mudd's pardon, which was granted by President Andrew Johnson in 1868.

On July 7, 1865, in the yard behind the Old Capitol Prison, Washington, D.C., Lewis Payne, David Herold, George Atzerodt, and Mary E. Surratt, found guilty of having conspired in the assassination of Abraham Lincoln were hanged less than 48 hours after death sentences were handed down by a nine-man military tribunal. Mary Surratt, mother of accused conspirator John Surratt (who evaded capture until late in 1866), owned the Washington boarding house in which Booth and six others planned the abduction of the president and, after that failed, his assassination. She was the first woman hanged in the United States.

on the very day that Kirby Smith, commanding the remaining fifty thousand men of the last Confederate army remaining in the field, surrendered to Union general Edward R. S. Canby.

Lewis Paine, David Herold, and George Atzerodt were all rounded up, tried, convicted, and sentenced to die, along with Mary Surratt, mother of another Booth conspirator, John Surratt, and owner of the Washington boardinghouse in which the Booth conspirators met. All except John Surratt (who was tried and acquitted in 1867) were hanged on July 7, 1865. Mary Surratt was the first woman to be executed by hanging in the United States.

Dr. Samuel Mudd, a Maryland physician who splinted Booth's broken leg early in his eleven-day flight from justice, was sentenced to life imprisonment but was pardoned by President Andrew Johnson in 1868 after he saved many lives during a prison epidemic.

Secretary of State William H. Seward recovered from his wounds and continued to serve in the cabinet of President Andrew Johnson. He is best remembered for purchasing Alaska from the czar of Russia in 1867, an act derided at the time as "Seward's folly."

Secretary Stanton clashed with Andrew Johnson, who tried to remove him from office. This action gave a hostile Radical Republican Congress an excuse to impeach Johnson. A single Senate vote in 1868 saved him from removal, but he served out the remainder of his term virtually without authority, chief executive in name only. As for Stanton, he surrendered his office on May 26, 1868, the day of Johnson's final acquittal, and returned to his private law practice. On December 24, 1869, four days after President Ulysses S. Grant appointed him to the United States Supreme Court, an office he had long coveted, Edwin P. Stanton died.

Officer John F. Parker, the Washington Metropolitan policeman who was absent from his post outside of the State Box at Ford's Theatre, was neither investigated nor reprimanded but instead continued to serve on the force.

Major Henry Rathbone married his fiancée, Clara Harris. In 1894, he murdered her because, he said, he was jealous of her love for their children. Found not guilty by reason of insanity, he was committed to an asylum, where he died in 1911. His last words were: "The man with the knife! I can't stop him! I can't stop him!"

The sanity of Mary Todd Lincoln was repeatedly questioned in the years following her husband's death, and in 1875 her only surviving son, Robert (her youngest, Tad, having died in 1871), managed to persuade a judge to commit her to a private sanatorium. Early the following year, another judge reversed the commitment. Released, the president's widow never lived down the public humiliation. She died in 1882 and was buried beside her husband at Oak Ridge Cemetery in Springfield, Illinois.

John Wilkes Booth murdered Abraham Lincoln to avenge the South—"I die for my country," he said—but the South was certainly the ultimate victim of the assassination. In his Second Inaugural Address, Lincoln had called on his fellow loyal citizens to act "with malice toward none, with charity for all . . . to finish the work we are in, to bind up the nation's wounds, to care for him

110

who shall have borne the battle and for his widow and his orphan, to do all which may achieve and cherish a just and a lasting peace among ourselves and with all nations." Now, in the absence of Abraham Lincoln, a bitter North and a vengeful Congress found within themselves very little charity and an abundance of malice. For this, the South, especially the black South, would suffer throughout the nineteenth century and well into the twentieth.

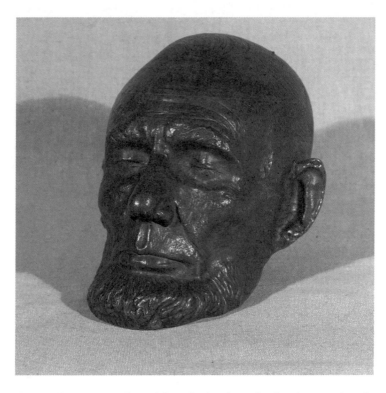

Among the many myths and legends that have developed concerning the assassination of Abraham Lincoln is that a death mask was made shortly after his assassination. In fact, there never was such a mask; however, two life masks were created, the first executed in Chicago by the sculptor Leonard Volk in April 1860, and the second, shown here, done by artist Clark Mills, in Washington, during February 1865. The Mills mask is in the collection of the Smithsonian Institution.

Anxious for some memento from the slain president, someone thought to remove a button from Lincoln's evening coat.

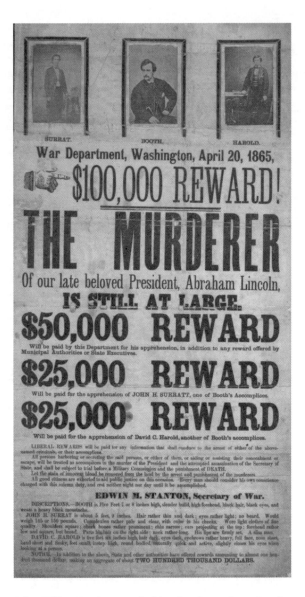

John Wilkes Booth was a fugitive for eleven days after the assassination of the president. This wanted poster, featuring likenesses of John H. Surratt, Jr., John Wilkes Booth, and David E. Herold, was widely circulated.

APPENDIX:

TEXT OF ARTICLES FOUND IN LINCOLN'S POCKETS AT THE TIME OF ASSASSINATION

Emancipation in Missouri.

SLAVERY TO CEASE TO EXIST JULY 4, 1870.

The Missouri State Convention adjourned yesterday, after having passed the following ordinance of emancipation by a vote of fifty-one ayes against thirty-six nays:

SECTION 1. The first and second clauses of the twenty-sixth section of the 3d article of the constitution is hereby abrogated.

SEC. 2. That slavery or involuntary servitude, except in punishment of crime, shall cease to exist in Missouri on the 4th of July, 1870, and all slaves within the state on that day are hereby declared to be free: Provided, however, that all persons emancipated by this ordinance shall remain under the control and be subject to their late owners, or their legal representatives, as servants during the following period, to wit: Those over forty years of age, for and during their lives; those under twelve until they arrive at the age of twenty-three; and those of all other ages until the 4th of July, 1876. The persons, or their legal representatives, who, up to the moment of emancipation, were owners of slaves hereby freed, shall, during the period for which the services of such freedmen are reserved to them, have the same authority and control over the said freedmen for the purpose of receiving the possessions and services of the same that are now held by the master in respect of his slaves; provided, however, that after the said 4th of July, 1870, no person so held to service shall be sold to non-residents or removed from the state by authority of his late owner or his legal representative.

SEC. 3. All slaves hereafter brought into the state and not now belonging to citizens of the state shall thereupon be free.

SEC. 4. All slaves removed by consent of their owners to any seceded state after the passage by such state of an act or ordinance of secession, and thereafter brought into the state by their owners, shall thereupon be free.

SEC. 5. The General Assembly shall have no power to pass laws to emancipate slaves without the consent of their owners.

SEC. 6. After the passage of this ordinance no slave in this state shall be subject to state, county or municipal taxes.

Governor Gamble announced the withdrawal of his resignation. He will, therefore, continue to serve as Governor until the election of his successor on the 18th of August, 1864.

The Disaffection Among the Southern Soldiers.

The Toledo (Ohio) Blade publishes, from the original copy now in possession of its editors, the following letter, which was picked up in the streets of Brandon, Mississippi, by Captain Dinnis, of the 62d Ohio Regiment. The Blade says that it is written in unusually fair penmanship, and is evidently the production of an intelligent man who is in a position to speak correctly of whereof he writes. It confirms other reports which we have recently had from the South of the demoralization and despondency of many of its soldiers:

BRANDON, July 16, 1863.

I wrote to you very hurriedly yesterday, and this morning learn that Gen. Johnston has ordered this army to be marched across to Enterprise, one hundred miles further. It will take a week longer. No provision has been made along the route, and the men are already much dissatisfied with the vacillating policy and hollow promises by which they have been duped so long.

Of the thirty thousand paroled at Vicksburg, only one half are now together, and ere we reach Enterprise this number will be reduced to five thousand—they of the Georgia, Alabama, and Tennessee troops, who also will leave with or without furloughs so soon as they learn the alternative of going into camp of parole. The army of the Mississippi is completely lost.

Meantime, Gen. Johnston holds Jackson—we hear the guns constantly. The enemy are making gradual approaches, and after a week longer will have that place. With it falls Mobile. This entire section is fleeing eastward. Georgia will have a population of five millions to feed this year. Ruin, utter and entire ruin, has swept over this State. The negro emancipation policy, at which we so long hooted, is the most potent lever of our overthrow. It steals upon us unawares, and ere we can do anything the plantations are deserted, families without servants, camps without necessary attendants, women and children in want and misery. In short, the disadvantages to us now arising from the negroes are ten-fold greater than have been all the advantages derived from earlier in the war.

It is useless to discuss the errors of the past—possibly there have been none that could have been avoided—certainly we are a defeated and a ruined people, shorn of our strength, powerless for a successful solution of the problem undertaken: or, rather ours was erroneous. The solution has been shown us by a more favored people.

John Bright on the Presidency.

John Bright, the "British Reformer," whose efforts in behalf of the United States, in combating the English sentiment in favor of the rebels, have awakened for him love and gratitude on the part of all loyal Americans, has written a letter to Horace Greely, in which, after alluding to the great struggle for liberty, in which we are now engaged, he says:

At this moment, we turn our eyes rather to the political than to the military struggle; and there is, with us, the same difference of opinion and of sympathy, as regards your upcoming Presidential election, that has been manifested in connection with your contest in the field.

All those of my countrymen who have wished well to the rebellion, who have hoped for the break-up of your Union, who have preferred to see a Southern Slave Empire rather than a restored and free Republic, so far as I can observe, are now in favor of the election of Gen. McClellan. All those who have deplored the calamities which the leaders of secession have brought upon your country, who believe that Slavery weakens your power and tarnishes your good name throughout the world, and who regard the restoration of your Union as a thing to be desired and prayed for by all good men, so far as I can judge, are heartily longing for the re-election of Mr. Lincoln. Every friend of your Union, probably, in Europe, every speaker and writer who has sought to do justice to your cause since the war began, is now hoping, with an intense anxiety, that Mr. Lincoln may be placed at the head of your Executive for another term.

It is not because they believe Mr. Lincoln to be wiser or better than all other men on your continent, but they think they have observed in his career a grand simplicity of purpose, and a patriotism which knows no change and which does not falter. To some of his countrymen there may appear to have been errors in his course. It would be strange indeed if, in the midst of difficulties so stupendous and so unexpected, any administration or any ruler should wholly avoid mistakes. To us, looking on from this distance, and unmoved by the passions from which many of your people can hardly be expected to be free— regarding his Presidential path with the calm judgment which belongs rather to history than to the present time, as our outside position enables us, in some degree, to regard it—we see in it an honest endeavor faithfully to do the work of his great office, and, in the doing of it, a brightness of personal honor on which no adversary has yet been able to fix a stain.

I believe that the effect of Mr. Lincoln's re-election in England, and in Europe, and indeed throughout the world, will be this: it will convince all men that the integrity of your great country will be preserved, and it will show that Republican institutions, with an instructed and patriotic people, can bear a nation safely and steadily through the most desperate perils.

PRESIDENT LINCOLN.

The large audience assembled last evening at the Academy of Music, to hear an address from Rev. Henry Ward Beecher, may be considered as fairly representing the most enlightened and intelligent population of Philadelphia. The welcome to Mr. Beecher was hearty, as it should have been. Every portion of his address was well received; but the loudest applause was given when he spoke in commendation of the course of the National Government in its prosecution of the war against the Southern rebels. An incidental allusion to General Jackson called forth some hearty plaudits. When they ceased Mr. Beecher, in his peculiar quiet way, said "Abraham Lincoln may be a great deal less testy and wilful than Andrew Jackson, but in a long race, I do not know but that he will be equal to him." The storm of applause that followed this seemed as if it would never cease. The turn given to the popular enthusiasm, by the mention of Lincoln's name alongside of Jackson's, was wholly unexpected. But the spontaneous outburst how strong a hold the President has upon the popular heart throughout the loyal North. As the time approaches for a new Presidential election, and people cast their eyes about for a candidate, there is no one so generally looked to as Abraham Lincoln. Other men may have the requisite talents and virtues; but none impress the people as being so well entitled to the next term of four years as the man who has so faithfully guided the republic through the terrible storms of civil war. There is a general feeling that after a term of war he is entitled to a term of peace; and that other men, military and civil, must defer their claims at least until the year 1868.

THE MESSAGE OF THE GOVERNOR OF MISSOURI.

We confess our inability to perceive in the message of the Governor of Missouri, the portions of which document that are of general interest we printed yesterday, any trace of that copperheadism or disloyalty so freely charged upon him by the radicals. He congratulates the State upon its pacification, upon the fact that there is no military organization within its borders hostile to the Government of the United States; and declares that "our chief duty is to support the Government with all our energies in its endeavors to suppress the rebellion in other States." That we understand to be loyal. It meets the case exactly. If there is any copperhead about it, we can't see it. The Ordinance of Emancipation Governor GAMBLE accepts "as a measure that will, in a brief period, accomplish the great object to be attained in making Missouri A FREE STATE." He believes it will go quietly into operation "and the State be relieved of all the evils of slavery." That don't seem to us to be a disloyal opinion. The Governor is also disposed to encourage the emigration of free laborers from Europe, and recommends a special appropriation to promote that object. If Governor GAMBLE were a Kentuckian we should think him a very sound Union man. We do not know but he would be charged with being an "Abolitionist." Slavery is dead in Missouri. That vast State, the geographical center of the Republic, may henceforth be set down as a free State. But the radicals are not satisfied with the death of slavery. Like the boy who pounded the dead snake, they want to "make it deader." And we have no objections to any blows inflcted [*TYPO IN ORIGINAL*] upon the institution. But because the President did not yield to demands of the radicals that seemed intolerant and obtrusive, he is charged by hundreds of furious journalists with deserting "the cause of freedom." The charge is unfounded and absurd. Doubtless he would rejoice as heartily as any radical, at the speedy abolition of slavery in Missouri, but he is not disposed to encourage excesses that might damage the good cause itself.

A Conscript's Epistle to Jeff. Davis.

The following quaint epistle has been furnished for publication by a member of the Mounted Rifles, who picked it up in a deserted rebel camp on the Chowan river, about thirty miles from Winton, while out on a scouting expedition last spring.

The letter was addressed in this wise:

Read, if you want to, you thieving scalp hunter, whoever you are, and forward, post paid, to the lord of high chancellor of the devil's exchequer (?) on earth.

JEFF. DAVIS, Richmond, Va.

HEADQUARTERS "SCALP HUNTERS,"

CAMP CHOWAN, N. C., Jan. 11.

Excellency Davis :

With feelings of undeveloped pleasure that an affectionate conscript intrusts this sheet of confiscated paper to the tender mercies of a Confederate States mail carrier, addressed, as it shall be, to yourself, O Jeff., Red Jacket of the Gulf, and Chief of the Six Nations—more or less. He writes on the stump of a shivered monarch of the forest, with the "pine trees wailing round him," and "Endymion's planet rising on the air." To you, O Czar of all Chivalry and Khan of Cotton Tartary, he appeals for the privilege of seeking, on his own hook, a land less tree—a home among the hyenas of the North. Will you not halt your "brave columns," and stay your gorgeous career for a thin space?—and while an admiring world takes a brief gaze at your glorious and God-forsaken cause, pen for the happy conscript a furlough without end? Do so, and mail it, if you please, and mail it to that city the windy, wandering, Wigfall didn't winter in, called for short Philadelphia.

123

The Etesian winds sweeping down the defiles of the Old Dominion, and over the swamps of Suffolk, come moaning through the pines of the old State, laden with the music, and sigh themselves away into sweet sounds of silence to the far-off South. Your happy conscript would go to the far-away North whence the wind comes, and leave you to reap the whirlwind, with no one but your father, the Devil, to rake and bind after you. And he's going.

It is with intense and multifariously proud satisfaction that he gazes for the last time upon our holy flag, that symbol and sign of an adored trinity—cotton, niggers and chivalry. He still sees it in the little camp on the Chowan, tied to the peak of its palmetto pole, and floating out over our boundless Confederacy, the revived relic of ages gone, banner of our king of few days and full of trouble. And that pole in its tapering uprightness testifying some of the grandest beauties of our nationality; its peak pointing hopefully toward the tropical stars, and its biggest end—run into the ground. Relic and pole, good bye. 'Tis best the conscript goes; his claim to chivalry has gone before him. Behind he leaves the legitimate chivalry of this unbounded nation centered in the illegitimate son of a Kentucky horse-thief.

But a few more words, illustrious President, and he is done—done gone.

Elevated by their sufferings and suffrages to the highest office in the gift of a great and exceeding free people, you have held your position without a change of base, or purpose of any sort, through weary months of war, and want, and woe; and though every conscript would unite with the thousands of loyal and true men in the South in a grand old grief at your downfall, so too will they sink under the calamity of an exquisite joy when you shall have reached that eminent meridian whence all progress is perpendicular.

And now, bastard President of a political abortion, farewell.

"Scalp hunters," relic, pole, and chivalrous confederates in crime, good-bye. Except it be in the army of the Union, you will not again see the conscript, NORM. HARROLD, of Ashe county, N.C.

SHERMAN'S ORDERS FOR HIS MARCH.

SPECIAL FIELD ORDERS—NO. 120.

HEADQUARTERS, MILITARY DIVISION OF THE MISSISSIPPI, IN THE FIELD, KINGSTON, Ga., NOV. 9, 1864.

I. For the purpose of military operations this army is divided into two wings, viz., the right wing, Maj. Gen. O. O. Howard commanding, the 15th and 17th corps; the left wing, Maj. Gen. H. W. Slocum commanding, the 14th and 20th corps.

II. The habitual order of march will be, whenever practicable, by four roads, as nearly parallel as possible, and converging at points hereafter to be indicated in orders. The cavalry, Brig. Gen. Kilpatrick commanding, will receive special orders from the Commander-in Chief.

III. There will be no general trains of supplies, but each corps will have its ammunition and provision train, distributed habitually as follows: Behind each regiment should follow one wagon and one ambulance; behind each brigade should follow a due proportion of ammunition wagons, provision wagons and ambulances. In case of danger, each army corps should change this order of march by having his advance and rear brigade unencumbered by wheels. The separate columns will start habitually at seven A.M., and make about fifteen miles per day, unless otherwise fixed in orders.

IV. The army will forage liberally on the country during the march. To this end, each brigade commander will organize a good and sufficient foraging party, under the command of one or more discreet officers, who will gather near the route traveled corn or forage of any kind, meat of any kind, vegetables, corn meal, or whatever is needed by the command; aiming at all times to keep in the wagon trains at least ten days provisions for the command and three days forage. Soldiers must not enter the dwellings of the inhabitants or commit any trespass; during the halt or a camp they may be permitted to gather turnips, potatoes and other vegetables, and drive in stock in front of their camps.

To regular foraging parties must be entrusted the gathering of provisions and forage at any distance from the road traveled.

V. To army corps commanders is entrusted the power to destroy mills, houses, cotton gins, &c., and for them this general principle is laid down: In districts and neighborhoods where the army is unmolested, no destruction of such property should be permitted; but should guerillas or bushwhackers molest our march, or should the inhabitants burn bridges, obstruct roads, or otherwise manifest local hostility, then army corps commanders should order and enforce a devastation more or less relentless, according to the measure of such hostility.

VI. As for horses, mules, wagons, &c., belonging to the inhabitants, the cavalry and artillery may appropriate freely and without limit; discriminating, however, between the rich, who are usually hostile, and the poor or industrious, usually neutral or friendly. Foraging parties may also take mules or horses to replace the jaded animals of their trains, or to serve as pack mules for the regiments or brigades. In all foraging, of whatever kind, the parties engaged will refrain from abusive or threatening language, and may when the officer in command thinks proper, give written certificates of the facts, but no receipts; and they will endeavor to leave with each family a reasonable portion for their maintenance.

VII. Negroes who are able-bodied and can be of service to the several columns, may be taken along; but each army commander will bear in mind that the question of supplies is a very important one, and that his first duty is to see to those who bear arms.

VIII. The organization at once of a good pioneer battalion for each corps, composed, if possible, of negroes, should be attended to. This battalion should follow the advance guard, should repair roads and double them if possible, so that the columns will not be delayed after reaching bad places. Also, army commanders should study the habit of giving the artillery and wagons the road, and marching their troops on one side; and also instruct their troops to assist wagons at steep hills or bad crossings of streams.

IX. Capt. O. M. Poe, Chief Engineer, will assign to each wing of the army a pontoon train, fully equipped and organized, and the commanders thereof will see to its being properly protected at all times.

By order of Maj. Gen. W. T. SHERMAN.

L. M. DAYTON, Aid de Camp.

The Two Platforms

LINCOLN AND JOHNSON.

Resolved, That it is the highest duty of every American citizen to maintain against all their enemies the integrity of the Union, and the paramount authority of the Constitution and laws of the United States; and that, laying aside all differences and political opinions, we pledge ourselves as Union men, animated by a common sentiment, and aiming at a common object, to do everything in our power to aid the Government in quelling, by force of arms, the rebellion now raging against its authority, and in bringing to the punishment due to their crimes the rebels and traitors arrayed against it.

Resolved, That we approve the determination of the Government of the United States not to compromise with the rebels, or to offer any terms of peace, except such as may be based upon an "unconditional surrender" of their hostility and a return to their just allegiance to the Constitution and laws of the United States, and that we call upon the Government to maintain this position and to prosecute the war with the utmost possible vigor to the complete suppression of the rebellion, in full reliance upon the self-sacrifice, the patriotism, the heroic valor, and the undying devotion of the American people to their country and its free institutions.

Resolved, That as slavery was the cause, and now constitutes the strength of the rebellion, and as it must be always and everywhere hostile to the principles of republican government, justice and the national safety demand its utter and complete extirpation from the soil of the Republic, and that we uphold and maintain the acts and proclamations by which the Government, in its own defence, has aimed a death-blow at this gigantic evil. We are in favor, furthermore, of such an amendment to the Constitution, to be made by the people in conformity with its provisions, as shall terminate and forever prohibit the existence of slavery within the limits of the jurisdiction of the United States.

Resolved, That the thanks of the American people are due to the soldiers and the sailors of the army and navy, who have periled their lives in defence of their country, and in vindication of the honor of the flag; that the nation owes to them some permanent recognition of their patriotism and valor, and ample and permanent provision for those of their survivors who have received disabling and honorable wounds in the service of the country; and that the memories of those who have fallen in its defence shall be held in grateful and everlasting remembrance.

Resolved, That we approve and applaud the practical wisdom, the unselfish patriotism, and unwavering fidelity to the Constitution and the principles of American liberty with which Abraham Lincoln has discharged, under circumstances of unparalleled difficulty, the great duties and responsibilities of the Presidential office; that we approve and endorse, as demanded by the emergency and essential to the preservation of the nation, and as within the Constitution, the measures and acts which he has adopted to defend the nation against its open and secret foes; that we approve especially the proclamation of emancipation, and the employment as Union soldiers of men heretofore held in slavery; and that we have full confidence in his determination to carry these and all other constitutional measures essential to the salvation of the country into full and complete effect.

Resolved, That we deem it essential to the general welfare that harmony should prevail in the national councils, and we regard as worthy of public confidence and official trust those only who cordially endorse the principles proclaimed in these resolutions, and which should characterize the administration of the Government.

Resolved, That the Government owes to all men employed in its armies, without regard to distinction of color, the full protection of the laws of war, and that any violation of these laws or of the usages of civilized nations in the time of war by the rebels now in arms should be made the subject of full and prompt redress.

Resolved, That the foreign emigration which in the past has added so much to the wealth and development of resources and increase of power to the nation, the asylum of the oppressed of all nations, should be fostered and encouraged by a liberal and just policy.

Resolved, That we are in favor of the speedy construction of the railroad to the Pacific.

Resolved, That the national faith pledged for the redemption of the public debt must be kept inviolate, and that for this purpose we recommend economy and rigid responsibility in the public expenditures, and a vigorous and just system of taxation; that it is the duty of every loyal State to sustain the credit and promote the use of the national currency.

Resolved, That we approve the position taken by the Government that the people of the United States never regarded with indifference the attempt of any European Power to overthrow by force, or to supplant by fraud, the institutions of any republican government on the western continent, and that they view with extreme jealousy, as menacing to the peace and independence of this our country, the efforts of any such power to obtain new footholds for monarchical governments, sustained by a foreign military force in near proximity to the United States.

M'CLELLAN AND PENDLETON.

Resolved, That in the future, as in the past, we will adhere with unswerving fidelity to the Union and the Constitution, and insist on maintaining our national unity as the only solid foundation of our strength, security, and happiness as a people, and as the framework of Government equally conducive to the welfare and prosperity of all the States, both Northern and Southern.

Resolved, That this convention does explicitly declare, as the sense of the American people, that, after four years of failure to restore the Union by the experiment of war, during which, under the pretence of military necessity, or the war power, higher than the Constitution, the Constitution itself has been disregarded in every part, and public liberty and private right alike trodden down, and the material prosperity of the country essentially impaired. Justice, humanity, liberty, and the public welfare demand that immediate efforts be made for the cessation of hostilities, with a view to an ultimate convention of all the States, or other peaceable means to that end, that, at the earliest practicable moment, peace may be restored on the basis of the Federal Union of the States.

Resolved, That the direct interference of the military authority of the United States in the recent elections held in Kentucky, Maryland, Missouri, and Delaware was a shameful violation of the Constitution, and a repetition of such acts in the approaching election will be held as revolutionary, and to be resisted with all the means and power under our control.

Resolved, That the aim and object of the Democratic party is to preserve the Federal Union and the rights of the States unimpaired; and they hereby declare that they consider Administrative usurpation of extraordinary and dangerous powers not granted by the Constitution; the subversion of the civil by military law in States not in insurrection; the arbitrary military arrest, imprisonment, trial, and sentence of American citizens in States where civil law exists in full force; the suppression of the freedom of speech and of the press; the denial of the right of asylum; the open and avowed disregard of State rights; the employment of unusual test oaths, and the interference with and denial of the right of the people to bear arms, as calculated to prevent a restoration of the Union, and the perpetuation of a Government "deriving its just powers from the consent of the governed."

Resolved, That the shameful disregard of the Administration in its duty in respect to our fellow-citizens who now are, and long have been, prisoners of war, in a suffering condition, deserves the severest reprobation and scorn alike of the public and common humanity.

SOURCES

Bishop, Jim. *The Day Lincoln Was Shot.* 1955; reprint ed., New York: Gramercy, 1983.

Clarke, Asia Booth. *The Unlocked Book: A Memoir of John Wilkes Booth by His Sister.* New York: Putnam, 1938.

Crook, William H. *Through Five Administrations.* New York: Harper and Brothers, 1907.

Hanchett, William. *The Lincoln Murder Conspiracies.* Urbana and Chicago: University of Illinois Press, 1983.

Helm, Katherine. *The True Story of Mary, Wife of Lincoln.* New York: Harper and Brothers, 1928.

Lamon, Ward Hill. *Recollections of Abraham Lincoln, 1847–1865.* Chicago: A. C. McClurg, 1895.

Leale, Charles A. *Lincoln's Last Hours: Address Delivered before the Commandery of the State of New York Military Order of the Loyal Legion of the United States.* New York: privately printed, 1909.

Lewis, Lloyd. *The Assassination of Lincoln: History and Myth.* 1929; reprint ed., Lincoln: University of Nebraska Press, 1994.

Steers, Edward, Jr. *Blood in the Moon: The Assassination of Abraham Lincoln.* Lexington: University Press of Kentucky, 2001.

Turner, Thomas Reed. *Beware the People Weeping: Public Opinion and the Assassination of Abraham Lincoln.* Baton Rouge: Louisiana State University Press, 1982.

PHOTO CREDITS

All photography courtesy of Library of Congress with the exception of the derringer image (78) and map (104) which are courtesy of the National Park Service.

The Gettysburg Address included in the kit was also courtesy of the Library of Congress. The Considerable scholarly debate continues about whether the Nicolay copy is the "reading" copy. In 1894 Nicolay wrote that Lincoln had brought with him the first part of the speech, written in ink on Executive Mansion stationery, and that he had written the second page in pencil on lined paper before the dedication on November 19, 1863. Matching folds are still evident on the two pages, suggesting it could be the copy that eyewitnesses say Lincoln took from his coat pocket and read at the ceremony.